HYSTERIA

or Fragments of an Analysis of an Obsessional Neurosis

Terry Johnson

**The Royal Court Writers Series published by
Methuen Drama in association with the Royal Court Theatre**

Royal Court Writers Series

Hysteria was first published in Great Britain
in the Royal Court Writers Series in 1993
by Methuen Drama
an imprint of Reed Consumer Books Ltd
Michelin House, 81 Fulham Road, London SW3 6RB
and Auckland, Melbourne, Singapore and Toronto
in association with the Royal Court Theatre
Sloane Square, London SW1N 8AS
and distributed in the United States of America
by Heinemann, a division of Reed Publishing (USA) Inc
361 Hanover Street, Portsmouth, New Hampshire NH 03801 3959

Reprinted 1993

Reprinted with corrections 1994

ISBN 0–413–68210–2

A CIP catalogue record for this book
is available from the British Library

The quotes from Dali in the programme are extracted from his
autobiography, *The Secret Life of Salvador Dali*, which is published
by Alkin Books Ltd.

Front cover photograph of Freud
courtesy of the Mary Evans Picture Library

Typeset by Hewer Text Composition Services, Edinburgh
Printed and bound in Great Britain by Cox & Wyman Ltd,
Reading, Berkshire

The Royal Court Theatre
in association with The Theatre of Comedy
Company, Stephen Evans and Karl Sydow
presents

or Fragments of an Analysis of an Obsessional Neurosis

by Terry Johnson

First performance at the Royal Court Theatre
on 26 August 1993

Financially assisted by the Royal Borough of Kensington and Chelsea
Recipient of an Arts Council Incentive Funding Award

Recipient of a grant from the Theatre Restoration Fund &
from the Foundation for Sports & the Arts

The Royal Court's Play Development Programme is
funded by the Audrey Skirball-Kenis Theatre

Registered Charity number 231242

Theatre Upstairs

12 - 16 October

The Royal Court Theatre in association with the Goethe-Institut and the Austrian Institute presents

Austria & Germany -
new plays in the 90's

a series of rehearsed readings introducing the very best new writers from Germany and Austria:

Tuesday 12th October
RABENTHAL
by **Jorg Graser** (translated by David McLintock)

Wednesday 13th October
SOLIMAN
by **Ludwig Fels** (translated by Anthony Vivis)

Thursday 14th October
IN DEN AUGEN EINES FREMDEN
(In the Eyes of a Stranger)
by **Wolgang Maria Bauer** (translated by Tom Beck)

Friday 15th October
TÄTOWIERUNG *(Tattooing)*
by **Dea Loher**
(translated by Sebastian Michael & Michael Cabon)
& A LIEBS KIND *(A Sweet Child)*
by **Harald Kislinger** (translated by Tom Beck)

Saturday 16th October
ALPENGLÜHEN *(Sunset in the Alps)*
by **Peter Turrini** (translated by Richard Dixon)

Saturday 16th October From 12 noon
WRITING FOR THE '90'S
a panel discussion *(free)*

Part of the Audrey Skirball-Kenis Playwrights Programme

Box Office
071 730 2554

THE AUDREY SKIRBALL-KENIS PLAYWRIGHTS PROGRAMME

Since it began in 1956, the aim of the English Stage Company has always been clear: to develop and perform the best in new writing for the stage. In our present climate it is more important than ever for the Royal Court to adhere to these principles of development which have proved so successful in the past. Hence the Audrey Skirball-Kenis playwright programme at the Royal Court.

*The **Audrey Skirball-Kenis Theatre** is a non-profit arts service organisation based in Los Angeles. Since its founding in 1989 the ASK Theatre has sought to contribute to the quality, growth and vitality of theatre through the development of new writing for the stage. This mandate is being accomplished by offering comprehensive programmes and support services which provide direct assistance to playwrights. The **Audrey Skirball-Kenis Playwrights Programme at the Royal Court** is unique in its transatlantic connection. Through various possible combinations of workshops, readings, dramaturgy, production without decor and commissioning, this new and creative programme exchange will provide the opportunity for generations of writers to share their innovative ideas, aesthetics and working methods. In doing so these aims will not only benefit the programme of work presented at the Royal Court in the future, but also nourish contemporary theatre, nationally and internationally.*

THE ENGLISH STAGE COMPANY

The English Stage Company was formed to bring serious writing back to the stage. The Court's first Artistic Director, George Devine, wanted to create a vital and popular theatre. In order to promote this, he encouraged new writing that explored subjects drawn from contemporary life as well as pursuing European plays and forgotten classics. When John Osborne's **Look Back in Anger** was first produced in 1956, and revived in '57, it forced British Theatre into the modern age. At the same time Brecht, Giraudoux, Ionesco and Sartre were also part of the repertoire.

The ambition to discover new work which was challenging, innovative and also of the highest quality became the fulcrum of the Company's course of action. Early Court writers included Arnold Wesker, John Arden, David Storey, Ann Jellicoe, N F Simpson and Edward Bond. They were followed by a generation of writers led by David Hare and Howard Brenton, and in more recent years, celebrated house writers have

included Caryl Churchill, Timberlake Wertenbaker, Robert Holman and Jim Cartwright. Many of their plays are now regarded as modern classics.

In line with the policy of nurturing new writing, the Theatre Upstairs has mainly been seen as a place for exploration and experiment, where writers learn and develop their skills prior to the demands of the Mainstage auditorium. Anne Devlin, Andrea Dunbar, Sarah Daniels, Jim Cartwright, Clare McIntyre, Winsome Pinnnock, and more recently Martin Crimp have, or will in the future, benefit from this process. The Theatre Upstairs proved its value as a focal point for new work with the production of the Chilean writer, Ariel Dorfman's **Death and the Maiden**. More recently, talented young writers as diverse as Jonathan Harvey, Adam Pernak, Phyllis Nagy (in association with the Liverpool Playhouse) and Gregory Motton (in association with the Royal National Theatre Studio) have been shown to great advantage in this space.

David Suchet and Lia Williams in **Oleanna** by David Mamet, 1993

1991, 1992, and 1993 have been record-breaking years at the box-office with capacity houses for productions of **Top Girls**, **Three Birds Alighting on a Field**, **Faith Healer**, **Death and the Maiden** (which moved to The Duke of York's), **Six Degrees of Separation** (which moved to the Comedy Theatre) and most recently **King Lear** and **Oleanna** (which has now moved to The Duke of York's). **Death and the Maiden** and **Six Degrees of Separation** won the Olivier Award for Best Play in 1992 and 1993 respectively. **Three Birds Alighting on a Field** has been awarded Best West End Play by the Writer's Guild of Great Britain, and has been successfully revived.

After nearly four decades, the Royal Court Theatre is still a major focus in the country for the production of new work. Scores of plays first seen in Sloane Square are now part of the national and international dramatic repertoire.

Katrin Cartlidge in **The Terrible Voice of Satan** by Gregory Motton, 1993

SIGMUND FREUD : A CHRONOLOGY

1856   *Born Moravia*

1860   *Family move to Vienna*

1876   *Studies chemistry, turns to physiology and anatomy. Moves to research, finally decides to study medicine*

1883   *Breuer remarks to Freud that neurotic behaviour was always connected to the secrets of the marriage bed*

1885   *Charcot emphasises that certain nervous disorders are always a question of "La chose genitale"*

            Chrobak asks Freud to take charge of a patient with a severe anxiety, whose husband was impotent and adds that the only cure for it could not be prescribed; repeated doses of a normal penis.

1886   *Starts practise as a neurologist*

            Marries Martha Bernays

1892   *Working with a series of hysterical patients, (mostly women from the professional classes), Freud originates psycho-analysis.*

            Slow evolution from Freud's original analytical methods (hypnosis, suggestion, forehead pressing and questioning) to free association methods begins. Fully established by 1895.

            "When sexual tension arises within the body attains a certain degree, it leads in the mind to sexual desire, libido, with various accompanying ideas and emotions; but when for any reason this natural process is checked, the tension is transformed into anxiety."

1894   *Publishes "The Defence of Neuro Psychoses".*

            "In hysteria it is chiefly sexual ideas (in women) that have proved unacceptable to the personality. Every hysteria is founded in repression, always with a sexual content."

            Freud: "He (Breuer) is entirely converted to my sexuality theory."

            Breuer: "I don't believe a word of it!"

            Breuer abandons him, unable to stomach the idea that hysterical symptoms could always be traced back to sexual trauma.

1895   *Publishes "Studies in Hysteria".*

1896   **Spring:**

            Publishes "The Aetiology of Hysteria".

            "The specific cause of all neuroses is some disturbance in the sexual life of the patient. More precisely, the cause in hysteria in a passive sexual experience before puberty, i.e. a traumatic seduction."

            "At the bottom of every case of hysteria will be found one or more premature sexual experiences, belonging to early childhood."

            Writes a letter to a medical theorist Wilhelm Fliess:

            "Have I revealed the great clinical truth to you, either in writing or by word of mouth? Hysteria is the consequence of presexual shock. Obsessional neurosis is the consequence of presexual pleasure later transformed into guilt."

            "I believe this to be a momentous revelation, the discovery of a caput nil of neuropathology."

            Autumn:

            Freud's father Jacob dies.

"By one of the obscure routes behind the official consciousness the old man's death affected me deeply. I valued him highly and understood him very well indeed, and with his peculiar mixture of deep wisdom and imaginative light-heartedness he meant a great deal in my life. By the time he died his life had been long over, but at death the whole past stirs within one."

1897   Freud identifies signs of psychoneurosis in his sister Marie.

Begins searing task of self-analysis. Works alone through the long summer family holiday. Begins to have grave doubts about his previous theory of Infantile Seduction.

1898   Publishes "Sexuality in the Aetiology of Neurosis" in which he asks himself;

"Could the imagined stories of seduction represent an unsuspected sexuality in very young children and a sexual desire for the parent, the memory of which had been lost to the adult mind by its suppression into the unconscious?"

Freud's Theory of Infantile Sexuality was born, and became the cornerstone of his future psychoanalytical work.

1908   The first international Congress of Psychoanalysis

1923   Diagnosed as suffering from cancer of the jaw

1936   Elected to the Royal Society

1938   **January:**

Freud arrives in London, escaping persecution in Vienna. Correspondence starts to arrive addressed to FREUD, LONDON

March:

Attends performance of Ben Travers' "Rookery Nook", Whitehall Theatre

Tries to get his sisters: *"four old women in their seventies"* out of Austria, but fails. (They die in concentration camps after his death.)

Visits from autograph hunters, cranks, lunatics, pious men with tracts, attempts to convert the unbeliever

July:

Salvador Dali visits for tea

November:

"Kristallnacht" in Germany.

In his final writings, expresses nagging doubts about some of the conclusions he reached during the years 1896-1899. (Some of these passages eventually to be excised by the Freud estate from future publications.)

1939   A broadcast speaks of the war to end all wars. Someone asks Freud if this would indeed be the last. *"My last war"* he replies.

Air raid sirens tested. Freud's bed moved into a safe downstairs room.

"I must be near death; they've stopped telling me my cigars will kill me."

Publishes "Moses and Monotheism"

23rd September, 3.00am:

Freud dies.

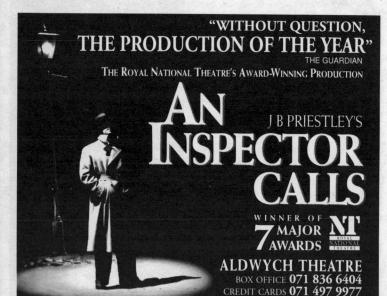

DALI

DALI AND FREUD

Dali made Freud reconsider his opinion that the surrealists were cranks; Freud spoke of his candid fanatical eyes and undeniable technical mastery. Freud professed to be interested investigating how a surrealist picture came to be painted;

'From the critical point of view it could be maintained that the notion of art defies expansion as long as the quantitative proportion of unconscious material and preconscious treatment does not remain within definite limits.'

Dali: 'I understand by the lesson of classic tradition of his old age how many things were at last ended in Europe with the imminent end of his life. He said to me;

'"In classic paintings I look to the sub-conscious; in a surrealist painting for the conscious."

'This was a pronouncement of a death sentence on surrealism as a doctrine, as a sect, as an ism. But it confirmed the reality of it's tradition as a state of the spirit; it was the same as in Leonardo - a "drama of style", a tragic sense of life and of aesthetics. At this moment Freud was occupying himself mainly with "religious phenomena and Moses." And I remember with what fervour he uttered the word "sublimation" on several occasions; "Moses is the flesh of sublimation."'

SEXUALITY

Dali: 'Heaven is what I have been seeking all along. The first time I saw a woman's depilated armpit I was seeking heaven. When with my crutch I stirred the putrefied and worm-eaten mass of my dead hedgehog, it was heaven I was seeking. When from the summit of Muli de la Torre I looked far down into the black emptiness, I was also and still seeking heaven.'

PHILOSOPHY

Dali: 'The individual sciences of our epoch have become specialized in these three eternal vital constants; the sexual instinct, the sense of death, and the space-time anguish. After their analysis, after the experimental speculation, it again becomes necessary to sublimate them. The sexual instinct must be sublimated into aesthetics; the sense of death into love; and the space-time anguish into metaphysics and religion. Enough of denying, one must affirm. Enough of trying to cure; one must sublimate! Enough of disintegration; one must integrate, integrate, integrate. Instead of automatism, style. Instead of nihilism, technique; instead of collectivism and uniformization; individualism, differentiation, and hierarchization; instead of experimentation, tradition. Instead of reaction or revolution; RENAISSANCE!'

SIGMUND FREUD, 1938. Photo reproduced courtesy of the **Freud Museum, London.**

HYSTERIA

or Fragments of an Analysis of an Obsessional Neurosis

by Terry Johnson

SIGMUND FREUD	**Henry Goodman**
JESSICA	**Phoebe Nicholls**
ABRAHAM YAHUDA	**David de Keyser**
SALVADOR DALI	**Tim Potter**

There are also a number of non-speaking characters - please see free cast sheet for performers' names

Director	**Phyllida Lloyd**
Designer	**Mark Thompson**
Lighting Designer	**Rick Fisher**
Sound Designer	**Paul Arditti**
Production Manager	**Iain Gillie**
Stage Manager	**Marie-Frances Dunn**
DSM	**Clare Smout**
ASM	**Ruth Beal**
Assistant Director	**Roxana Silbert**
Costume Supervisor	**Jennifer Cook**
Voice Coach	**Julia Wilson-Dickson**
Set built by	**Miraculous Engineering**
Cloths painted by	**Chris Clark**
Set painted by	**Francis Coleman**
Poster/Leaflet Image	**Ralph Steadman**
Poster Design	**Sightlines**
Leaflet Design	**Loft**

There will be one interval of fifteen minutes

BIOGRAPHIES

TERRY JOHNSON

For the Royal Court: Insignificance, Cries from the Mammal House

Other plays include: *Imagine Drowning* (Hampstead); *Tuesday's Child* (Theatre Royal, Stratford East); *Unsuitable for Adults* (Bush); *Bellevue* (Welfare State International); *Days Here So Dark* (Paines Plough); *Amabel* (Bush).

Television includes: *99 To 1*, *Way Upstream* (adaptation, also directed), *Tuesday's Child* (with Kate Lock), *Time Trouble* (also directed). Film screenplays include: *Insignificance*, *Somebody Else*, *Aquarium*.

PAUL ARDITTI

For the Royal Court: Search and Destroy.

Other Theatre sound designs include: *The Winter's Tale*, *Cymbeline*, *The Tempest*, *Antony and Cleopatra*, *Entertaining Strangers*, *Coming In To Land*, *The Trackers of Oxyrhynchus* (Royal National Theatre); *The Gift of the Gorgon* (RSC & Wyndhams); *Orpheus Descending* (Haymarket & Broadway); *A Streetcar Named Desire* (Bristol Old Vic); *The Winter's Tale* (Manchester Royal Exchange); *The Wild Duck* (Phoenix); *Henry IV*, *The Ride Down Mount Morgan* (Wyndhams); *Born Again* (Chichester Festival Theatre); *Three Sisters*, *Matador* (Queen's); *Twelfth Night*, *The Rose Tattoo* (Playhouse); *Becket*, *Cyrano de Bergerac* (Haymarket); *Four Baboons Adoring the Sun* (Lincoln Center, New York, 1992 Drama Desk Award).

Opera Sound Designs include: *Gawain* (Royal Opera House).

Television Sound Designs include: *The Camomile Lawn*.

DAVID DE KEYSER

For the Royal Court: The Shawl and Prairie du Chien.

Other Theatre includes: *Duet for One* (Bush & Duke of York's); *The Archbishop's Ceiling*, *Principia Scriptoraie* (RSC); *Down an Alley Filled with Acts* (Mermaid); *The Big Knife* (Apollo); *Another Time* (Wyndhams); *Making it Better* (Hampstead & Criterion).

Television includes: *Madigan*, *Disraeli*, *Collision Course*, *Duet for One*, *Yes Prime Minister*, *The London Embassy*, *Out of the Shadows*, *Confessional*, *Bergerac*, *The House of Eliott*, *Between the Lines*, *Poirot*, *Berlin Break*, *Under the Hammer*.

Films include: *Golda*, *King David*, *Yentl*, *Doctor Fischer of Geneva*, *The Ploughman's Lunch*, *A Touch of Class*, *Catch Us if You Can*, *Leo the Last*, *A Dry White Season*, *Red King White Knight*, *Leon the Pig Farmer*.

RICK FISHER

For the Royal Court: King Lear, Three Bird Alighting on a Field (1991 & 1992), Six Degrees of Separation (& Comedy), Serious Money (& Wyndhams & Broadway), Bloody Poetry, Rose English (Barclays New Stages), A Mouthful of Birds, A Rock in the Water.

Other Theatre lighting designs include: *The Coup, Black Snow, Peer Gynt* (Royal National Theatre); *An Inspector Calls* (Royal National Theatre & Aldwych - 1992 Olivier Award Nomination for Best Lighting Design); *Misha's Party, Artists and Admirers, All's Well That Ends Well, The Virtuoso, The Alchemist, 'Tis Pity She's a Whore, Temptation, Restoration, Two Shakespearian Actors* (RSC); *Gift of the Gorgon* (RSC & Wyndhams); *Some Americans Abroad* (RSC & Broadway); *Much Ado About Nothing* (Queen's); *A Walk in the Woods* (Comedy); *Uncle Vanya* (Renaissance).

Opera lighting designs include: *La Boheme, L'Etoile, Peter Grimes* (Opera North); *Manon Lescaut* (Dublin); three seasons at Batignano, Italy. Dance lighting designs include: *The Kosh, Adventures in Motion Pictures*.

HENRY GOODMAN

For the Royal Court: Downfall.

Theatre in Britain includes: *Angels in America, After the Fall, Cat on a Hot Tin Roof, Beatrice & Benedict* (Royal National Theatre); *They Shoot Horses, Don't They, Every Man in his Humour, Henry V, The Devils, Redstar, Comedy of Errors, Volpone, The Time of Your Life, Astonish Me, Jacques & His Master, Henry VIII* (RSC); *City of Angels* (Prince of Wales); *Kvetch* (King's Head & Garrick); *Assassins*

(Donmar - 1993 Olivier Award for Best Performance in a Musical); Lady Sings the Blues, A Free Country (Tricycle). Theatre in South Africa includes leading roles in: Merchant of Venice, Tartuffe, Metamorphosis, The Government Inspector, Decadence, A Day in the Death of Joe Egg, Peter Pan, What the Butler Saw, Candide, Oliver!

Television includes: Lovejoy, Rides, Spinoza, 3 Up 2 Down, Maigret, The Gravy Train II, Zorro, El C.I.D., Gentlemen and Players, London's Burning, This is David Lander, Bust, After the War, The Chain, Old Flames, Columbus. Films include: Secret Weapon, Queen of Hearts, Son of The Pink Panther.

PHYLLIDA LLOYD

For the Royal Court: Six Degrees of Separation (& Comedy), An Arranged Marriage, The Burrow, Inventing a New Colour (co-production with Bristol Old Vic).

Other Theatre includes: What the Butler Saw, Much Ado About Nothing, A Midsummer Night's Dream, Insignificance, Every Black Day (Everyman, Cheltenham); The Comedy of Errors, A Streetcar Named Desire, Dona Rosita the Spinster, Oliver Twist (Bristol Old Vic); The Winter's Tale, The School for Scandal, Death and the King's Horseman, Medea (Manchester Royal Exchange); The Virtuoso, Artists and Admirers (RSC). Opera includes: L'Etoile, La Boheme (Opera North).

PHOEBE NICHOLLS

Theatre includes: An Inspector Calls, Pravda (Royal National Theatre); Three Sisters (Queen's); The Seagull (Lyric, Hammersmith); The Beautiful Part of Myself (Palace Theatre, Watford); The Cherry Orchard (Chichester Festival Theatre); Whose Life is it Anyway? (Mermaid).

Television includes: Secret Orchards, Brideshead Revisited, Blade on the Feather, Take Two, A Harmless Vanity, All For Love, Bouncing Back, Poppyland, Hay Fever, Gentry, Drowning in the Shallow End, Tell Me More. Films include: The Elephant Man, The Missionary, Ordeal by Innocence, Maurice, Heart of Darkness.

TIM POTTER

Theatre includes: Psycho, A Streetcar Named Desire, Citizen Kane, Apocalypse Now, Fall of the House of Usher, The Birthday Party (Acme Acting Company); Jonne Donne Show (Northcote Theatre, Exeter); Victims of Duty (Theatre Space); Dog Beneath the Skin, The Wizard of Oz (Half Moon); Tale of Two Cities (Glasgow Citizens); Salomé, Accidental Death of an Anarchist, The Sea (Royal National Theatre).

Television includes: Walter and June, Videostars, Luna, Angels in the Annexe, I Woke Up One Morning, Dead Head, Titus Andronicus, Ties of Blood, Wild Things, Blood Rights, Underbelly, Witchcraft, My Sister-Wife, Kinsey, Lovejoy. Films

include: Vroom; Salomé's Last Dance.

MARK THOMPSON

For the Royal Court: Six Degrees of Separation (& Comedy)

Other Theatre designs include: The Wind in the Willows, The Madness of George III (1991 Olivier Award for Best Set Design), Arcadia (Royal National Theatre); Measure for Measure, The Wizard of Oz, Much Ado About Nothing, The Comedy of Errors (1992 Joint Olivier Award for Best Set Design & 1992 Olivier Award for Best Costume Design) (RSC); Jumpers, The Country Wife, Mumbo Jumbo, The School for Scandal (Manchester Royal Exchange); Owners (Young Vic); Scarlet Pimpernel (Chichester Festival Theatre & Her Majesty's); Cabaret, Much Ado About Nothing, Ivanov (Strand Theatre); A Little Night Music (Chichester Festival Theatre & Piccadilly); Shadowlands (Queen's & Broadway); Volpone, Betrayal, Party Time (Almeida); Joseph & His Amazing Technicolor Dreamcoat (Palladium & Canadian, American and Australian tours - 1992 Joint Olivier Award for Best Set Design).

Opera & ballet designs include: Don Quixote, Il Viaggio a Reims (Covent Garden); Falstaff (Bremer Theatre, Germany & Scottish Opera); Peter Grimes (Opera North); Ariadne auf Naxos (Salzburg); Montag aus Licht (La Scala - costumes).

THE OLIVIER BUILDING APPEAL

The Royal Court reached the ripe old age of 100 in September 1988. The theatre was showing its age somewhat, and the centenary was celebrated by the launch of the Olivier Appeal, for £800,000 to repair and improve the building.

*Laurence Olivier's long association with the Court began as a schoolboy. He was given "a splendid seat in the Dress Circle" to see his first Shakespeare, **Henry IV Part 2** and was later to appear as Malcolm in **Macbeth** (in modern dress) in a Barry Jackson production, visiting from the Birmingham Repertory Theatre in 1928. His line of parts also included the Lord in the Prologue of **The Taming of the Shrew**. This early connection and his astonishing return in **The Entertainer**, which changed the direction of his career in 1957, made it natural that he should be the Appeal Patron. After his death, Joan Plowright CBE, the Lady Olivier, consented to take over as Patron.*

We are now three-quarters of the way to our target. With the generous gifts of our many friends and donors, and an award from the Arts Council's Incentive Fund, we have enlarged and redecorated the bars and front of house areas, installed a new central heating boiler and new air conditioning equipment in both theatres, rewired many parts of the building, redecorated the dressing rooms and we are gradually upgrading the lighting and sound equipment.

With the help of the Theatre Restoration Fund, work has now been completed on building a rehearsal room and replacing the ancient roofs. The Foundation for Sport and the Arts have promised a grant which will enable us to restore the faded Victorian facade of the theatre. So, much is being done, but much remains to do, to improve the technical facilities backstage which will open up new possibilities for our set designers.

Can you help? A tour of the theatre, including its more picturesque parts, can be arranged by ringing Becky Shaw on 071 730 5174. If you would like to help with an event or a gift please ring Graham Cowley, General Manager, on the same number.

'Secure the Theatre's future, and take it forward towards the new century. For the health of the whole theatrical life of Britain it is essential that this greatly all-providing theatre we love so much and wish so well continues to prosper.'
Laurence Olivier (1988)

Laurence Olivier 1907-1989
Photo: Snowdon

THE ROYAL COURT THEATRE

DIRECTION

Artistic Director
Max Stafford-Clark

Artistic Director Designate
Stephen Daldry

Casting Director
Lisa Makin

Literary Manager
Robin Hooper

Associate Director (Education)
Elyse Dodgson

Associate Director
James Macdonald

Literary Associate
Stephen Jeffreys*

Assistant Directors
Mary Peate
Roxana Silbert

Secretary
Katherine Jones

PRODUCTION

Production Manager
Bo Barton

Chief Electrician
Johanna Town

Deputy Chief Electrician
Matthew O'Connor

Electrician
Denis O'Hare*

Master Carpenter
Guy Viggers

Deputy Master Carpenter
David Berry

Technical Manager, Theatre Upstairs
Chris Samuels

Sound Designer
Paul Arditti

Sound Operator
Julie Winkles*

Wardrobe Supervisor
Jennifer Cook

Deputy Wardrobe Supervisor
Glenda Nash

*= part time

The Assistant Directors receive bursaries from The Gerald Chapman Trainee Director Fund, BBC Television and the Arts Council.

ADMINISTRATION

General Manager
Graham Cowley

Assistant to General Manager
Rebecca Shaw

Finance Administrator
Mark Rubinstein

Finance Assistant
Rachel Harrison

Marketing & Publicity Manager
Guy Chapman

Press (071-730 2652)
Anne Mayer

Sales Manager
David Brownlee

House Manager
Candice Brokenshire

Deputy House Manager
Dafydd Rogers

Box Office Manager
Richard Dyer

Deputy Box Office Manager
Heidi Fisher

Box Office Assistants
Matthew Hendrickson
Peter Collins*

Lunch Bar Caterer
Andrew Forrest*

Stage Door/Reception
David Curry*
Michael Warburton*

Evening Stage Door
Tamsin Dodgson*
Tyrone Lucas*

Maintenance
John Lorrigio*

Cleaners
Eileen Chapman*
Maria Correia*
Mila Hamovic*

YOUNG PEOPLE'S THEATRE

Director
Dominic Tickell

Writers Tutor
Andrew Alty*

Youth Drama
Moira Arthurs

Schools and Community Liaison
Celine Corbin

Special Projects
Carl Miller

ENGLISH STAGE COMPANY

President
Greville Poke

Vice Presidents
Joan Plowright CBE
Sir Hugh Willatt

COUNCIL

Chairman
John Mortimer QC, CBE

Bo Barton
Stuart Burge
Anthony Burton
Harriet Cruickshank
Stephen Evans
Sonia Melchett
James Midgley
Winsome Pinnock
Richard Pulford
Timberlake Wertenbaker
Nicholas Wright
Alan Yentob

ADVISORY COUNCIL

Diana Bliss
Tina Brown
Allan Davis
Elyse Dodgson
Robert Fox
Jocelyn Herbert
Michael Hoffman
Hanif Kureishi
Jane Rayne
Ruth Rogers
Jim Tanner
Kathleen Tynan

PATRONS

Diana Bliss
Gwen Humble
Ian McShane
John Mortimer
Richard Pulford
Irene Worth

CORPORATE PATRONS

Carlton Communications
Copthorne Tara Hotels
Penguin Books Ltd
Simons Muirhead and Burton
William Verry Limited

ASSOCIATES

Barclays Bank plc
Henny Gestetner
Nick Hern Books
Greville Poke
Richard Wilson

For Marion

Characters

Sigmund Freud   An energetic old man with startling eyebrows. He has cancer of the jaw, but this should only affect his speech at the end of the play.

Jessica   A woman in her late twenties or early thirties.

Abraham Yahuda   A large man in his sixties. An even greater weight and status than Freud.

Salvador Dali   A small or tall Spaniard with a strange moustache and a talent for painting.

The style of playing varies as Freud's last thoughts, recent memories and suppressed anxieties dictate the action.

Depending on the resources of the theatre, other actors may make a brief appearance in Act Two.

Note: This is the corrected script of the play.

Setting

1938

Sigmund Freud's study at 20 Maresfield Gardens, Hampstead, London. A large, high-ceilinged room plastered in pastel-blue. The room is furnished richly: dark oaks and mahogany.

US french windows lead to a narrow porch, and beyond, a well-kept garden.

USR the door to a closet. SR a large desk. DSR a wood-burning stove.

Along the wall SL, an armless analysis couch covered with a rich Moroccan rug and half a dozen cushions. On the wall above, another beautiful rug. Just beyond the head of the couch, a comfortable tub chair.

DSL the door to the rest of the house.

There are bookshelves holding fine embossed volumes, and every available surface holds antiquities from Ancient Greece, Rome, Egypt and the Orient. The vast majority of these are small human figures in pottery, wood and bronze.

The setting should be naturalistically rendered to contrast with the design challenge towards the end of Act Two.

Act One

Scene One

A shaft of light rises to isolate **Freud** *asleep in the tub seat. His eyes open and he stares steadily at a large dark* **Figure** *downstage. (In fact* **Yahuda***, but featureless, a primordial, paternal presence.)*

The **Figure**'s *hands move under the sharp glare of an anglepoise lamp. A hypodermic syringe and a phial glint as he fills one from the other.*

He approaches **Freud** *and as he does, we hear the growing sound of human turmoil; people shoving, shouting, hundreds of people, a sense of urgency, even panic.*

The **Figure** *dwarfs* **Freud***. We are aware now of the enormous, paralysing tension in* **Freud***. An unbearable pain has met an immovable object.*

The **Figure** *injects* **Freud***. A train engine whistles, then the sound of a steam train pulling out of a station washes over the voices and obliterates the hubbub . . . shouts of departure make way for the powerful, demanding noise of the train.*

Freud *suddenly relaxes as the morphine hits. The train noise becomes a gentle, reassuring clatter, like a lullaby.*

The **Figure** *leaves. The lights slowly change, the train subsides.*

Freud*'s study. Night. Rain beyond the windows.*

Freud asleep in the tub chair. Wakes and looks at his watch. A long silence.

Freud If you are waiting for me to break the silence you will be deeply disappointed. The silence is yours alone, and is far more eloquent than you imagine.

He turns in his chair and looks towards the couch. Double-takes when he sees there is no one on it. Looks around the room. Opens the door, peers out, closes the door. Goes to his desk. Hesitantly presses the buzzer on an unfamiliar Bakelite intercom.

Freud Anna?

Anna (*a voice pulled from sleep*) Yes, father?

Freud She's gone.

Anna Who, father?

Freud Where's she gone?

Anna Where's who gone?

Freud It's um . . .

Looks at his watch.

Anna What is it?

Freud Ten to.

Anna It's ten to five. It's the middle of the night.

Freud There was a girl.

Anna Have you slept yet?

Freud I had a patient.

Anna Maybe you dreamed her.

Freud I don't dream patients, I dream surgeons and publishers.

Anna Go to bed, father.

Freud The nights are valuable.

Anna Yahuda will be here for lunch, and you've an appointment with Mr Dali immediately after.

Freud I'll sleep in the morning. What's this thing?

In front of his face hangs an electric light pull; a four-foot cord with a brass knob on the end.

Anna What thing?

Freud This thing hanging here in front of me. This thing in my hand.

Anna Um . . .

Freud It's just dangling here. It's got a nob on the end.

Anna Mm hm?

Freud What is it?

Anna I've . . . no idea.

Freud What am I supposed to do with it?

Anna Shall I call the nurse?

Freud Shall I give it a pull?

Anna No, just . . . leave it alone, father.

He pulls it. The lights go out.

Freud *Scheisse!*

Anna Father?

Freud The lights have gone out.

Anna Oh . . . that!

Freud Damn thing.

Anna It's a light pull.

Freud I know what it is; what's it doing here?

Anna Ernst put it up this afternoon.

Freud I can't see a thing.

A crash of falling objects.

Anna Father?

Freud I hate the dark.

Anna You should be asleep.

Freud I know what's in it.

Anna You need more, not less, as time passes.

Freud The body maybe. The mind more than ever craves . . .

He switches on the light.

Freud Illumination.

Anna Shall I come down?

Freud No, I'm fine.

Anna Goodnight then.

Freud Goodnight.

He switches off the intercom. Some of the antique figures on his desk have been knocked over; he rights them. He picks up his pen to write. Nothing comes. He gets up and lies on the couch.

Freud I have been preparing, somewhat unsuccessfully, for my death which Yahuda would have me believe is imminent. I am inclined to agree with his diagnosis, but this morbid preparation is . . . difficult. I have never liked waiting for trains; standing on the platform looking back down the track: never a glance, of course, in the direction of one's destination. Like all the trains I ever caught, this one is running late. And so I wait. I rearrange the luggage at my feet; I unfold and refold my newspaper, failing to find anything of interest, even though the headlines roar. And over and over I mentally rehearse the panic of boarding, check my watch with the clock, grow anxious and inexplicably . . . impatient. I prepare and prepare and yet remain unprepared, because when the train arrives there is never time to button the jacket or check the ticket or even say a meaningful goodbye. So until my inevitably fraught departure, all I can do is wait, and rearrange the luggage.

His eyes have closed.

A pause, then a figure appears through the rain and stops outside the french windows. **Jessica** *is sopping wet and initially appears waif-like. She wears a thin mackintosh. Her hair hangs dripping to her shoulders.*

She taps on the glass. **Freud** *opens his eyes. She taps again. He rises, disorientated, and discovers the source of the noise. She smiles.*

Freud Go away. Go away. This is a private house, not Madame Tussauds. I admit I found it flattering when I arrived, this English passion for standing and staring, but I'd rather be melted down, thank you, than have any more thumbnails surreptitiously pressed into my flesh, so please . . . go away! Oh very well, stay where you are, catch your death for all I care. What do you want?

He goes to his intercom. She raps frantically. He doesn't press the buzzer. She speaks. We don't hear her through the glass.

Jessica I have to speak to you.

Freud What?

Jessica I have to speak to you.

Freud I can't hear you. Go away.

Very matter-of-fact, she takes out a cut-throat razor and holds it to her wrist.

Jessica I have to speak to you.

Freud *looks away. Thinks. Then goes to the french windows and unlocks them. He steps back. She enters.*

Freud Stop there! Stop.

She stops. Closes the razor. Offers it to him. He takes it and secures it in a drawer.

Jessica I wasn't sure you'd let me in.

Freud You're sopping wet.

Jessica It's raining.

Freud That rug is from Persia.

Jessica You told me to stop.

Freud Get off the rug.

She steps forward.

Freud No closer. Step sideways. To the left. Stand there.

Jessica Here?

Freud Good.

Jessica Good.

Freud How did you get into the garden?

Jessica I climbed. Where the elm rests on the wall.

Freud I'll have a tree surgeon to it first thing in the morning.

Jessica Grazed my knee; look.

Freud What are you, some sort of insomniac student?

Jessica No.

Freud You want me to read something you wrote?

Jessica No.

Freud Are you inebriated, irresponsible, rich? Is this a dare?

Jessica No.

Freud Do you know who I am?

Jessica Oh yes.

Freud Then what do you want?

Jessica I don't know. I haven't yet decided.

Freud Who are you?

Jessica Don't you recognise me?

Freud It feels as though I should.

Jessica Yes, you should.

Freud We've met?

Jessica No, never.

Freud Please. It's late. Who are you?

Jessica I am your Anima, Professor Freud.

Freud My what?

Jessica It's a psychological term denoting the denied female element of the male psyche.

Freud I know what it is.

Jessica Denied but desired.

Freud Damn nonsense, that's what it is. Did *he* send you?

Jessica Who?

Freud The Lunatic. Jung the crackpot, friend of the gods?

Jessica No.

Freud He did, didn't he? This is his feeble idea of a practical joke.

Jessica No one sent me.

Freud Due to my advancing years I am quite prepared to come up against the odd figment of my own imagination, but I have no time for flesh-and-blood imposters. And I certainly refuse to confront aspects of my personality I did not even propose! Anima is tosh. Archetypes are a theatrical diversion!

Jessica I've not read much Jung.

Freud Not much is too much. How long have you been in the garden?

Jessica All night. Watching the house. The lights going out. Then one last light, illuminating you.

Freud Perhaps you should sit. Judging from your behaviour so far you are either dangerously impulsive or pathologically unhappy.

Jessica That's true.

Freud Which?

Jessica Both, I think. I have inverted morbid tendencies, I know. And a great deal of free-floating anxiety desperate for someone to land on. I am mildly dysfunctional, yes.

Freud You have recently been in analysis?

Jessica No, I've recently been in a library.

Freud What do you want of me?

Jessica Later.

Freud There is no later. If you are looking for a doctor, I'm afraid I have to disappoint you. I cannot take any more patients. Those I see now will soon be abandoned. I cannot add to my unfinished business.

Jessica What if I were desperate?

Freud There would be no point; I could never conclude. I will give you the name of a good man.

Jessica No.

Freud My health deteriorates daily. There are others now more able than I . . .

Jessica No. It's you I must see.

Freud Then you must be disappointed. I shall call someone to show you out.

Jessica Don't do that.

Freud It's very late. I'm an old man.

Jessica What's wrong with your mouth?

Freud With this half, nothing. The other half I left in Vienna.

Jessica How careless of you.

Freud It's in a jar of formaldehyde. The surgery was drastic, but advisable.

Jessica I think I'd rather die than have a piece of me removed.

Freud Cancer cells develop a passionate urge to replicate. They abandon any concern for the function of their familial organ and strike out to conquer foreign tissue. They undermine the natural state, absorb and conquer! They are the National Socialists of human meat; best left, I felt, in Austria. Now, you must go.

Jessica It's still raining.

Freud How could you possibly get any wetter? Please.

Jessica I'm cold.

Freud I'm not unsympathetic, but if you want to get warm, get home.

Jessica I have no home.

Freud I must insist. This is improper.

Jessica I'll show you improper.

She takes off her coat.

Freud What are you doing?

She takes off her dress.

Freud Please, I am perfectly aware you wish to gain my attention but this is highly inappropriate. I shall call my daughter.

Jessica And how will you explain me?

Freud There is nothing to explain.

Jessica Naked and screaming?

Freud She will understand.

Jessica But will the inhabitants of West Hampstead?

Freud Now stop this. Your behaviour is totally unacceptable!

Jessica My behaviour, Professor Freud, is as you first diagnosed. It is desperate, as am I!

She goes into the garden, still undressing.

Freud Come back inside!

Jessica Do I start screaming or will you give me an hour of your precious time?

Freud I will not be blackmailed. Come out of the rain.

Jessica No. I shall stand here until I'm too wet to think. Too cold to care.

Thunder.

Freud *takes her coat and pursues her. Brings her back inside, wrapped.*

Freud Sit.

He moves a chair nearer the stove and ushers her into it.

Jessica Thank you. I'm sorry.

She cries.

Freud I shall try to help. But could we please remember this is my study, not some boulevard farce.

Jessica This isn't your study. Your study was in Vienna.

Freud Who are you?

Jessica Is it the same?

Freud Almost. In the Bergasse it wasn't as simple to walk out into the garden.

Jessica Why?

Freud I was on the second floor. And there were many more books.

Jessica More?

Freud I had to choose between books and the survivors.

Jessica Who?

Freud The figures.

Jessica They're beautiful.

Freud And were buried, unseen, for centuries. It would have been criminal to inter them again. It felt bad enough cramming them into rail crates for transportation. Each of them is quite unique but packed in side by side, they lose their individual identities. Wrapped in newsprint they become . . . faceless.

Jessica Are you in pain?

Freud Yes. Are you?

Jessica Oh yes.

Freud Intermittent?

Jessica Constant. I thought there were drugs.

Freud I prefer to think in pain than dream in oblivion.

Jessica I dream in pain.

Freud I cannot take you on. I have no . . . time. You understand.

Jessica It won't take long.

Freud Would that were true.

Jessica It won't. I know what's wrong with me.

Freud Self-analysis is rarely successful.

Jessica You did it.

Freud I had the advantage of being me.

Jessica And you were all you had to go on. I've read your books. All of them.

Freud Have you really?

Jessica Yes.

Freud Understand much?

Jessica Most.

Freud Hmph.

Jessica I didn't much enjoy *Jokes and Their Relationship to the Unconscious*. If you were going to analyse jokes you might have chosen a couple that were funny. I suspect you've no sense of humour.

Freud Nonsense. Only last week I was taken to the theatre and I laughed three or four times.

Jessica What at?

Freud I believe it was called *Rookery Nook*.

Jessica Doesn't prove you've a sense of humour; proves you've a complete lack of taste.

Freud It had a seductive logic, and displayed all the splendid, ha!, anal obsessions of the English.

Jessica Frankly, some of your concepts are funnier than your jokes.

Freud For instance?

Jessica Penis envy, for instance. How in a thousand years of civilised thought anyone could imagine a penis an object of envy is beyond me. Those I have seen erect and bobbing seem positively mortified at their own enthusiasm. The only one I ever saw flaccid looked like something that had fallen out of its shell. Euugh! Why would anyone envy a squidgy single-minded probiscus that thinks it's God's special gift to those without.

Freud You say you've done no analysis?

Jessica None.

Freud I think you should begin as soon as possible.

She lies on the couch.

Freud But not with me. Tomorrow afternoon I will refer you. Until then, you must let me sleep.

Jessica I'll be fine.

Freud You can't stay here.

Jessica Don't pretend you're not curious, Professor. You're longing to know what brought me here. There's nothing you'd like better than to see me barefoot in the head.

Freud You are mistaken.

Jessica Please.

Freud If I were to listen to anything you had to say, I would do so only because you are obviously disturbed, and only on the understanding that what we were doing was an assessment pending a referral.

Jessica All right.

Freud Very well.

He sits at the head of the couch.

Jessica How do we start?

Pause.

Jessica I can't see you.

Pause. She twists around. He looks at her with a well-practised neutral expression.

Jessica That's the point, is it? That's part of it?

She lies back. Pause.

Jessica And silence? Is that part of it too? It is, isn't it? How many minutes of silence must you have endured?

Sunrise happens; a shaft of red light and a burst of birdsong.

Jessica I don't know how to begin. I was born in Vienna twenty-nine years ago. I am an only child. My mother was beautiful, my father was the owner of a small printworks and a temple elder. We lived in a tall, narrow house. It had four floors but not many more rooms; a strange house, as if built by a child, an unsteady tower of wooden bricks. My father had a bad hip; he couldn't climb stairs. He had a room made up in what was the parlour. This was his room, at the bottom of the house. Anyway, I grew. I grew up, as you can see.

Freud *makes a note.*

Jessica You made a note, I heard you scribble.

She twists around.

Jessica What did you write, what did I say?

She gets the same neutral expression.

Jessica I see. Well anyway, here I am. Should I talk about now or then? Past or present? Both, I know, I'm sure, but which end should I begin?

She rubs briefly at the top of her breast, as if removing a splash of wine. A hysterical manifestation.

Jessica Why am I here? I'm here because I was sent. I wouldn't have come of my own accord. I have been married two years and my husband is concerned for me. I would find it flattering if it were not. . . . He worries about my appetite, which is small, but does not concern me. I eat no more than I desire. My husband also wishes I spent more time outdoors; I prefer it inside. It is merely a preference, not an illness. So that's why I'm here. It is desired that I eat like a horse and live like one too, in a field if possible. If you could turn me into a horse my husband would be overjoyed.

She rubs.

Jessica What has he told you?

She gags.

Freud Would you like some water?

Jessica No thank you. Don't stand up. I don't like the outdoors, and I don't need three enormous meals a day.

Freud How long have you felt this way?

Jessica A year. Maybe longer. Yes. Nearly two. It's always longer than I remember.

Freud When did it start?

Jessica It developed. Nothing sudden, nothing . . .

She rubs. Shakes her stiff fingers.

Jessica One just becomes happier staying indoors, and less interested in the taste of food. Really, I wouldn't be here at all if it weren't for my wretched husband.

Freud What is wrong with your hand?

Jessica Didn't he tell you? The fingers of my hand. My hand has been examined by specialists; neither could explain the problem with my fingers.

Freud What is the problem?

Jessica We thought arthritis, but we're assured otherwise. These three fingers have grown stiff, you see. They bend at the joints but will not move apart. The hand still functions. I can use it. But it looks so . . . reptilian. It is intensely frustrating.

Freud And there is no physiological impairment?

Jessica None, I'm assured.

She gags, then rubs.

Jessica I'm sorry. Don't stand up. Well? Can you help me?

Freud No. I cannot.

Jessica I'm sorry?

Freud It is now certainly time for me to go to my bed.

Jessica That was hardly a full consultation, Professor; we're barely beyond the symptoms.

Freud I am as aware of the symptoms as you. And I am aware of the aetiology of your hysterical paralysis, as well as the traumatic triggers of your anorexia and agoraphobia.

Jessica So soon?

Freud I know these things not because your compulsive behaviour is unconvincing or because I am capable of completing an analysis in less than ten minutes, but because I published the facts of this case thirty years ago, and you no doubt, judging by your excellent knowledge of them, read it only recently. Now I am very tired, both of your games and of this evening . . .

Jessica Please, don't call anyone.

Freud Either you leave, this instant, or I'll wake the house.

Jessica It was a stupid thing to do. I'm sorry.

Freud What do you take me for?

Jessica It's a case history that interests me, that's all.

Freud So you are a student?

Jessica Yes. Yes, I am.

Freud Then your methods of study are most unorthodox.

Jessica May we discuss the case of Rebecca S?

Freud Certainly not. You disturb me, you attempt to deceive me . . .

Jessica Did I?

Freud What?

Jessica Deceive you?

Freud Not for very long.

Jessica I did though, didn't I? The gagging and the . . .

She rubs.

Jessica Was that how she . . . ?

Freud I was very explicit in my descriptions. You were very accurate in your impersonation.

Jessica Spooky.

Freud Now if you've had your fun . . .

Jessica Listen. I know I'm a fool. But Rebecca means a lot to me. She's the basis of my thesis. Please.

Freud You have an incredible nerve. I responded in good faith to your hysterical dishonesty. Had you chosen a less deceitful path to my door we may have had something to discuss. As it is you have forfeited any right to my time and attention. This is my final word. Now you may go into the garden and scream or dance with the spring fairies, I care not.

Jessica What would Dr Jung say if he heard you mention fairies?

Freud He'd probably take me down the path and attempt to introduce us. Now go home.

Jessica I have no home.

Freud Enough.

Jessica Please . . .

Freud Not one more word.

Jessica I'll go then.

Freud Good.

Jessica Could I ask one thing of you?

Freud One thing.

Jessica Could you lend me a pair of wellingtons?

Freud Wellingtons.

Jessica My feet are freezing. No, it's too much to ask. I'm sorry; I'll be fine.

Freud Wait there.

Jessica No really, I couldn't.

Freud It's a small price.

Jessica A pair of socks would be heaven; those thick sort of woolly ones.

Freud *leaves.*

Jessica's *manner changes. She goes to the filing cabinet and rifles through it. A door noise off. She pulls out a maroon file and hurries. She opens the french windows wide, then hides in the closet.*

Freud *returns, with boots and walking socks, to find her gone. Stands at the french windows for a while, until his confusion turns to philosophical acceptance. He closes the windows and leaves his study, switching off the light.*

Jessica *comes out of the closet. Turns on the anglepoise. Takes a journal out of her coat pocket, and carefully puts it on the desk.*

She opens the file, finds flimsy carbon copies of correspondence.

Settles down to work her way through the correspondence; a concentrated, obsessive search . . .

Lights fade.

Scene Two

Late afternoon. **Jessica** *has gone, as have the wellingtons. The room is reasonably tidy.*

Door opens and in marches **Yahuda**, *an elderly Jewish doctor. He clutches a visiting bag and a bound document.* **Freud** *follows.*

Yahuda No, no, no. I'm not here to debate with you. No one in your family, no friend, colleague or critic has ever convinced you you were wrong about anything. I'm quite happy to be argued into my grave, but I'm not about to be argued into yours. I did you the courtesy of reading this . . . babble, now will you do me the courtesy of listening.

Yahuda *stops at a chessboard in play and takes a move he's already prepared.*

Freud I had wondered at your silence during lunch.

Yahuda Being polite has given me indigestion. We are both old men.

Freud Time is short.

Yahuda I shall allow your ill-health to temper my anger, but not to lessen my resolve. I shall not leave this room until you have agreed not to publish this work.

Freud My friend . . .

Yahuda That remains to be seen.

Freud I see.

Yahuda The first paragraph made my blood run cold. 'If Moses was an Egyptian . . .'

Freud If.

Yahuda You do not mean the if, Freud. None of your ifs are questions; all your ifs are excuses for the outrageous statements they precede. Your proposal is that the man who gave us the word of God, the founder of the Jewish nation, was an Egyptian aristocrat.

Freud A simple reading of the facts . . .

Yahuda You deny his origins . . .

Freud Any intelligent analysis . . .

Yahuda You undermine the core of the myth!

Freud Myth, precisely.

Yahuda The symbolic expression . . .

Freud The reflection of an inner desire . . .

Yahuda Of a basic truth . . .

Freud A perversion of truth, an attempt to satisfy . . .

Yahuda Moses was a Jew! Moses was chosen! If Moses was not a Jew, then we were not chosen! He was a Jew as I am a Jew. And you?

Freud I have never denied, ever denied . . .

Yahuda Well, deny Moses and you deny us! At this time, of all times.

Freud Yes.

Yahuda When the little we have is being wrenched from us.

Freud I know.

Yahuda At this most terrible hour . . .

Freud I take away our best man.

Yahuda This is dreadful stuff. It is irreligious, unforgivably ill-timed, badly-argued piffle.

Freud But apart from that, what did you think?

Yahuda There can be no discussion. You may not publish.

Freud *takes a move on the chessboard.*

Freud Yahuda, you are a scholar. A believer I know, but a scholar all the same. And you do not believe that the Red Sea parted . . .

Yahuda The this and that of the event . . .

Freud Or that a babe floated down a river in a basket . . .

Yahuda Are lost in the mist, the history. The mystery . . .

Freud A babe in a basket would have drowned as sure as our nation on the ocean floor.

Yahuda The myth, Freud.

Freud You know these things for what they are.

Yahuda The myth is what's important.

Freud Have you been talking to the lunatic?

Yahuda Remove the essence of the myth and you undermine the foundation of our faith; you lead us to an agnostic hell. As indeed you seem intent on doing. Here. Right here. 'The undeniable power of faith can be explained away like any other neurotic compulsion.' 'Religion is the neurosis of humanity.'

Freud It's not a new idea.

Yahuda You presume to find no evidence of God but in the heads of men. In the imaginings of desperate minds. And what is a mind, according to your people? Sparks in the brain.

Freud And a little history.

Yahuda Well, God is more than meat and electricity. Or the suffering of a child. Or the arrogance of a traitor Jew.

Freud What alternative are you suggesting? That I censor my last thoughts, have them held in trust against a day when some other man, as he surely will, reaches the same conclusions and is told; well, there was someone else in darker times who thought the same as you. No, God is no more light in this darkness than a candle in a hurricane; eventually he will be snuffed out. But if one man's denial can explode him then that tiny conflagration would be a light far brighter than the guttering hopes he kindles in us. The death of

God would light us not to hell or heaven, but to ourselves. Imagine. That we begin to believe in ourselves.

Yahuda Damn yourself if you must.

Freud I have to publish.

Yahuda But remember one thing.

Freud What?

Yahuda You are not the only Jew who will die this year.

The pain **Freud** *has been suppressing overwhelms him. He fights and defeats it.*

Yahuda Sigmund? Are you in pain?

Freud Most uncalled for.

Yahuda I shall examine you.

Freud We both know what you'll find.

Yahuda Fetch a towel. A man in your condition should be making peace with his God and his fellow man. Not denying one and outraging the other.

Freud *goes to the closet.*

Freud I have spent my life standing up for unpleasant truths . . .

He opens the closet. An arm comes out and gives him a towel.

Freud Thank you.

He closes the door.

Freud . . . But it has never been my desire to offend . . .

Stops. Realises. Looks back.

Yahuda Know this, Freud. Unless you reconsider, you lose my friendship.

Freud Good God.

Yahuda Harsh, I know, but there it is.

Freud Get out.

Yahuda No need to be offensive.

Freud No, not you.

Yahuda Then who?

Freud What?

Yahuda You said; 'get out!'.

Freud Indeed. Get out . . . your things. Get your things out of your bag. And please, examine me.

Freud *sits and positions an anglepoise over his mouth.* **Yahuda** *takes an instrument from his bag, and peers into* **Freud**'s *mouth.*

Yahuda Be certain of one thing; there is precious little I would not do to prevent your publishing. If you had the clap I'd hang the Hippocratic oath and seriously consider blackmail. But not you of course. Guiltless. Half a century of meddling in other people's passions, countless female patients lying there in front of you, and never a whisper of impropriety. No scantily clad secrets in your closet, more's the pity. Oh, for a scandalous lever to prize you off your pedestal.

Freud Ont ee ihiculoh.

Yahuda What?

Freud Nothing.

Yahuda That certain things are hidden from us . . .

Freud Ot?

Yahuda Does not deny their existence.

Freud Ot hings?

Yahuda The minds of men, the face of God. You devote yourself to one invisible thing yet refuse to contemplate the other.

Finishes the examination.

Yahuda It's as you thought.

Freud Inoperable?

Yahuda It's very deep now. I'm sorry.

Freud No, if I had a God to thank, I would.

Freud *grimaces.*

Yahuda That's me prodding around. A pressure bandage?

Freud Thank you

Yahuda *removes from his bag a bicycle pump, a puncture repair outfit and an inner tube.*

Freud What do you intend doing with that?

Yahuda Mend my bike. Of course . . . Two centigrammes of morphine . . .

Freud No.

Yahuda Just the one?

Freud Absolutely not.

Yahuda Sooner or later.

Freud No.

Yahuda *ties the bandage tight around* **Freud**'s *jaw, with a bow on the top of his head.*

Yahuda It's hard watching even a stubborn irreligious fool like you make his way to a self-defined oblivion.

Freud I cannot end with an act of disavowal.

Yahuda Then end in silence.

Yahuda *moves to the closet.*

Freud No!

Yahuda What?

Freud Don't go in there.

Yahuda I need to wash my hands.

Freud Please. Use the one across the hall. This we use now as a closet. So much correspondence, so many books . . .

Yahuda Hmmph.

Yahuda *heads for the door. Stops on his way to examine the chessboard. Almost takes a move, but stops himself.*

Yahuda You think everyone but you is a complete fool.

Exits.

Freud *rushes to the closet and flings open the door.*

Freud You said you were going, I thought you were gone.

Jessica *appears wearing her raincoat and wellingtons.*

Jessica Get rid of your visitor, Professor. We have work to do.

Freud We have no such thing. I have other appointments.

Jessica Cancel them.

Freud I said I would arrange a referral.

Jessica *goes back into the closet.*

Freud Would you please come out of there! Very well, you give me no choice . . .

He steps towards the closet.
The raincoat hits him full in the face.

Freud My God.

Yahuda *enters through the other door.*

Freud *closes the closet door.*

Yahuda I left my bike in the garden. I'll fix the puncture then I'll be off.

Freud Good.

Yahuda And you've another visitor; some Spanish idiot with a ridiculous moustache. Dilly, Dally?

Freud Dali.

Yahuda Doolally by the look of him.

Freud The painter.

Yahuda Really? If you want a physician's advice, you're not up to it. You should be resting, not entertaining foreigners.

Freud A favour for a friend.

Yahuda Whose is that? (*Raincoat.*)

Freud Mine.

Yahuda Is it raining?

Freud Usually.

Yahuda Looks all right to me.

Freud The forecast was ominous.

Yahuda Indoor storms imminent?

Freud Yes. No. A possibility of flash flooding.

Yahuda Damn. I'll bring my bike inside.

Freud No.

Yahuda I can't mend it in the rain.

Freud It's not raining.

Yahuda You said it was just about to.

Freud No, I said there was the possibility of some weather. They weren't precise as to which sort.

Yahuda Looks awfully small for you.

Freud It shrank.

Yahuda When the last flash flood came thundering through your study, I suppose?

Freud Why don't you bring your bike through and mend it in the hall?

Yahuda As you wish. Though upstairs might be best.

Freud Upstairs?

Yahuda To eliminate any danger of sudden drowning.

Yahuda *exits though the windows.* **Freud** *opens the closet to return the coat.*

Freud Now please, I must insist that you come out of the closet.

Jessica Whatever you say . . .

Freud No. I mean, stay where you are, put your clothes back on and then . . .

A wellington boot flies out, which he catches.

Freud Please. You must modify this behaviour immediately. This is a childish and ineffectual form of protest since I haven't a clue what you're protesting *about*.

Jessica's *arm appears from the closet. Between her fingers, a letter of* **Freud**'s. *He moves until it's in front of his face, and starts to read it.*

Freud I don't understand.

She stuffs the letter right down into the boot. **Yahuda** *re-enters pushing his bike and walking on one heel.*

Freud *closes the closet.*

Yahuda You're overrun by snails; they're all over the path. I've trodden on half a dozen.

Freud Please, the rug.

Yahuda Could you take this for a second?

He hands the bike to **Freud**. *It is covered in snails and has a hot water bottle tied to the handlebars.*

Yahuda Where's your bootscraper?

Freud We don't have a bootscraper.

Yahuda This is England, for heaven's sake.

Freud And every bootscraper I encounter sends me flying into or out of someone's bloody conservatory!

Yahuda I'll find a stick or something. (*A crunch.*) There goes another one!

Yahuda *exits.*

Freud *puts the wellington on the floor and uses his free hand in an attempt to retrieve the carbon copy.*

Yahuda What the devil? Freud! What's this?

Freud *rises, his arm inside the boot.*

Yahuda *re-enters, hopping. He has only one shoe on.*

Freud What's what!

Yahuda I don't know what you call the damn things. It was in the middle of your lawn.

Standing on one leg, he holds up **Jessica**'s *slip. It falls in front of him.*

Dali (*off*) No no no! Is alright! I see myself!

A sharp knock on the other door. Enter **Dali***. A surprised pause, then sheer delight.*

Dali So. Is true. What Dali merely dreams, you live!!

Freud I can assure you there's a perfectly rational explanation.

Dali He does not wish to hear it.

Freud Who?

Dali Dali.

Freud Of course. Tell your Mr Dali I shall see him in just a few minutes.

Dali But he is here.

Freud I'm aware of that.

Yahuda And there's more of it, underwear and all sorts.

Freud It must have blown off the line. I'll be a few minutes.

Dali No, but he is here.

Yahuda There is no line.

Freud I know he's here, I heard you the first time. Ask him to wait a few minutes.

Yahuda Whose is it?

Dali But wait he cannot. He is here.

Freud Look dammit . . .

Dali I am he.

Freud Oh, I see.

Yahuda I'll put it on the compost.

Freud No! Give it to me.

Yahuda It's not yours, is it?

Freud Yes. No. It's . . . my daughter's.

Yahuda Anna's? At her age she should be dressing for warmth.

He drapes the slip over **Freud***'s arm and turns.*

Freud You are he.

Dali And he is honoured.

A crunch.

Yahuda Oh shit. There goes another one.

Yahuda *exits on his heel.*

Dali *rises, sits, pulls out a pad.*

Dali You will not object?

Freud What?

Dali A first impression.

Freud Ah.

Dali *sketches.*

Freud It's not my bike. And my physician has piles, thus the . . . (*Hot water bottle.*) As for the snails . . .

Dali Dali is passionate with snails.

Freud For, you mean.

Dali For, with, Dali's passions knows no bounds.

Freud They just . . . took a liking to the bike I suppose.

Dali You have a head like a snail.

Freud Thank you very much.

Yahuda *re-enters with a clean shoe and more clothing.*

Yahuda You want the rest?

Freud Yahuda, this is um . . .

Dali Dali.

Yahuda We met in the hall. Has Anna lost a lot of weight in the last week?

Dali You suffer from piles.

Yahuda How extraordinarily acute of you.

Dali Dali suffers also.

Yahuda I know; I've seen your pictures.

Dali You do not like the work of Dali?

Yahuda You want a frank answer?

Dali Always.

Yahuda I find your work explicitly obscene, deliberately obtuse, tasteless, puerile and very unpleasant to look at.

Dali What is not to like in this?

Yahuda I think I'll leave you to it, Freud.

Dali This is the man; the only man who can fully appreciate the genius of Dali's spontaneous method of irrational cognition and his critical interpretative association of delusional phenomena. Wait.

Exits.

Yahuda You want some advice?

Freud What?

Yahuda Don't let him get on the couch.

Dali *enters with a finished canvas. 'Metamorphosis of Narcissus'.*

Dali Is for you. Now you tell me. Look closely, and tell me . . . from what does Dali suffer?

Freud Eyesight?

Dali Is true. This man is genius.

Yahuda Excuse me, I have an operation to perform.

Freud Please, don't feel you have to . . .

Yahuda No, no. I'm sure you two have much to discuss. Here.

Offers **Freud** *a bundle of underwear.*

Freud Thank you.

Yahuda I'm damned if I can imagine her in them. In fact I'm grateful I can't imagine her in them. I'll see you when he's gone.

Exit **Yahuda** *with his bike.* **Dali** *resumes his sketch.*

Freud I'd really rather you didn't.

Dali A thought, an idea from your head, it belongs to you. But your image belongs to Dali. Please.

Freud I must insist. Put your pencil away.

Dali You neither do not like the work of Dali?

Freud Not if I am to be the subject. If I'd known this was your intention . . .

Dali Please. Dali has no intentions, only intent.

He puts his pad down.

Dali I have come to salute you . . .

Freud Please don't bother.

Dali . . . on behalf of all true disciples of the critical–paranoiac school of paint.

Freud Who are they?

Dali Dali. He is the only true disciples.

Freud I see.

Dali You are held in great esteem. We, by which I mean Dali and I, are engaged in a great struggle to drag up the monstrous from the safety of our dreams and commit to the canvas. It is you who have inspired this.

Freud I am most flattered.

Dali You say to dream, and there to search . . . is what I do. You say paranoia it transform reality to conform with the unconscious obsession, yes? So Dali gazes; is turned to stone, but and an egg. Narcissus flowers from the egg. Desiring to be reborn he only gazes at himself and dreams of death. Life in this state is as unlikely as a flower from an egg. Expressed with masterly technique and ingenious illusion of course, and this is what Dali does, and only him. Would you like me to hang him?

Freud Oh please, don't bother yourself.

Dali Is no bother. Is an honour. I put it here.

Freud That's a Picasso.

Dali Picasso is Spanish. (*Removes painting.*) So is Dali.

Freud You like Picasso?

Dali Picasso is genius. (*Tosses painting.*) So is Dali.

Freud I much admire 'Guernica'.

Dali Picasso is Communist.

Freud Yes.

Dali Neither is Dali.

Freud You'll have to forgive me for being frank. I am in a certain amount of pain.

Dali Divine.

Freud Distracting. It's been a pleasure to meet you.

Dali No. Dali cannot go. Not so soon. Let me describe to you the painting I have just completed. It is called . . . 'Dream Caused By The Flight Of a Bee Around a Pomegranate One Second Before Waking Up'. It depicts the splitting of a pomegranate and the emergence of a large gold fish. From the mouth of the fish leaps a tiger. From the mouth of the tiger leaps . . . another tiger. From the mouth of this tiger, a rifle with fixed bayonet about to pierce the white flesh of a naked girl, narrowly misses her armpit. Beyond all this a white elephant with impossible legs carries past a monument of ice.

Pause.

Dali You have to see it for yourself, really.

Freud Again, forgive my lack of courtesy . . .

Dali Please, have none.

Freud Very well. I have always thought the surrealist movement a conspiracy of complete fools. But as you had the audacity to elect me some sort of patron saint, I thought it only polite to meet you. I now find I lack the energy even to be polite.

Dali Excellent! Dali has no concern for your health, no desire to be liked, and no manners. Creatures who live in the shell, Dali eats. Until the moment he dies, he does as he please. And he refuses to leave.

Freud I don't think I've ever met a more complete example of a Spaniard.

Dali Do you mind if I examine your room?

Freud Yes.

Dali But I must.

Dali *looks around the room. Very nosey. Almost opens closet.*

Freud I suppose the war has brought you to England?

Dali In Spain until one week ago, Dali paint and is contemptuous of the Fascist machine rolling towards. Then he thinks; no, this is all getting too historical for Dali. Immediately the desire to leave is enormous, and acted upon immediately.

Freud Have you any idea when the desire to leave here might become at all substantial?

Dali When Dali, being here with you, no longer feels real to Dali.

Freud Shouldn't take too long then?

Dali Please. Your life is almost over. Don't waste your precious time trying to analyse Dali; he is completely sane. In fact, the only one.

Dali *finds a snail on* **Freud***'s desk. Unsticks it, pulls it from its shell and eats it.*

Dali It's not good. What sort of snail is this?

Freud English garden.

Swallows it.

Dali Is tasteless. Typical English.

Freud *looks for and finds another snail, which he deposits in a wastepaper bin. This becomes a running joke.* **Dali** *continues to look around, arrives at the closet and opens the door.* **Freud** *looks up.*

Freud N . . . er . . .

Dali *looks inside the closet and turns to stone. He closes the door, goes to* **Freud** *at the desk. Leans on the desk. Opens his mouth, closes it. Goes back to the closet. Opens it, goes inside, closes door behind him. A muffled blow, a cry and a crash.* **Dali** *emerges holding his genitals. Unable to speak for some time.*

Dali The girl in your closet.

Freud Yes?

Dali A hallucination, no?

Freud No? I mean, girl? What girl?

Dali In the closet.

Freud There's a girl in my closet?

Dali Naked girl.

Freud Nonsense. She must be a figment of your unique imagination.

Dali She kick me in the phallus.

Freud An impressive hallucinatory sensation.

Dali I have pain in the testicle.

Freud Hysterical.

Dali No, is not funny.

Freud Obviously you are at the peak of your imaginative powers.

Dali You think?

Freud *leads him to the door.*

Freud Your fantasies have grown so undeniable, they push through the fabric of reality. It is imperative you return home and paint at once.

Dali A naked girl in the closet of Freud with the hooves of a stallion; is good.

Freud Visionary.

Dali I shall dedicate to you.

Freud Thank you, goodbye.

Dali The pain is transformed; is divine.

Freud So good to have met you.

Dali The honour, it is Dali's. I owe you my life.

Freud An unintentional gift, I assure you.

Dali Goodbye!

He leaves. **Freud** *grabs the clothing and has his hand on the closet door handle when* **Dali** *re-enters.*

Dali No, no, no, no, no! I cannot leave.

Freud *hides the clothing behind his back*

Freud Please, be firm in your retholution. Resolution.

Dali Dali is firm in his trousers. His pain has transformed, his member tumescent. Dali is obsessed. The vision in the closet must be his. He must look again.

Freud No.

Enter **Yahuda**. **Freud** *spins.*

Yahuda Anna's? I think not. Give them to me.

Freud The what?

Yahuda The flimsies.

Freud I don't have them.

But **Dali** *can see them, and pounces.*

Dali Ahah! The garments of the Goddess.

He takes the bundle and buries his face.

Yahuda Has he met your daughter?

Dali She is a feast; you smell.

Yahuda *takes the bundle.*

Yahuda I'll do no such thing. Freud, there's about enough silk here to cover Anna's left shin. I intend to confront her with these.

Freud Ah.

He heads for the door.

Yahuda And you'd better hope for a positive identification.

Freud No, Yahuda . . . !

Dali She fill my senses!

He throws off his jacket, grabs his pad, and opens the closet.

Freud No!

Freud *rushes for the closet,* **Yahuda** *escapes. Closet door closes behind* **Dali** *before* **Freud** *can get there. He rushes to the other door, but it closes behind* **Yahuda**.

A pause. **Freud** *eyes the closet. Vague Spanish mumblings from within.*

Freud *approaches the door, curious. Puts his ear to it. As he straightens, the door flies open, hitting him on the jaw.* **Dali** *hurtles out, trips and lands spectacularly, out for the count.*

Jessica (*off*) I am a defenceless woman and refuse to be intimidated by amorous Spaniards!

Freud His arousal is entirely your responsibility.

Jessica A woman has the right to sit naked in a cupboard without being propositioned.

Freud I would defend your right, but not your choice of cupboard. Should this man sadly regain consciousness, I can give you no guarantee of his behaviour unless you get dressed.

Jessica Very well; give me my clothes.

Freud Ah.

Jessica (*off*) What does that mean? Ah?

Freud I have temporarily mislaid them.

Jessica Then you'll have to take me as I come.

Freud No! Wait. Here.

Throws her **Dali**'*s jacket.*

Jessica Thank you.

Freud All right?

Jessica Well, I don't think I'll get into the royal enclosure.

Freud Please, stay hidden.

Jessica If you swear to give me a hearing.

Freud All right, I swear.

Jessica When?

Freud When Yahuda's gone. I'll give two knocks.

He closes the door. It opens again.

Jessica It's bloody cold in here; I want more clothes.

Freud All right! All right! I'll get you some. Just wait quietly.

Freud *closes the door on her again. Lifts* **Dali**'s *head, looks in his eyes. Drops his head and starts to remove his trousers.*

Enter **Yahuda**.

Yahuda She's never seen them in her life.

He sees **Freud** *and* **Dali***. Pause.*

Yahuda You and I have to have a serious chat.

Freud I was just . . . removing his trousers.

Yahuda So I see. He appears to be unconscious.

Freud Exactly. He began hyperventilating and fainted. I'm loosening his clothing.

Yahuda He breathes through his backside as well, does he?

Freud He was complaining of abdominal pains.

Yahuda Really?

Yahuda's *professionalism takes over. He examines* **Dali***.*

Freud Most definitely. Indigestion maybe, but perhaps something very serious. Hopefully a ruptured appendix.

Yahuda Hopefully!?

Freud Well I mean, something worth you rushing him to hospital for, but of course hopefully not, touch wood.

Raps twice on the nearest bit of wood, which happens to be the closet door. **Jessica** *comes out of the closet.* **Freud** *steers her back in and closes the door, stubbing her elbow.*

Jessica Ow.

Freud Ow. That was the sound he made, just before he collapsed.

Yahuda *rises.*

Dali Owwww.

Yahuda This man has suffered a blow to the head.

Freud Yes. He's very tall. On his way to the garden, he hit his head on the top of the doorframe.

Yahuda As he fainted?

Freud Yes.

Yahuda Which?

Freud Both.

Yahuda That's not possible.

Freud Yes it is. He was standing on the filing cabinet, fainted, and hit his head on the way down.

Yahuda What was he doing on the filing cabinet?

Freud I don't know. I wasn't here. I was already in the garden.

Yahuda Doing what?

Freud Chasing a swan.

Yahuda Where did that come from?

Freud I haven't the faintest idea. But it could have been the swan that entered the room very aggressively and forced Dali to retreat to the filing cabinet where he fainted in terror.

Yahuda This is utter nonsense.

Freud The answer is a sponge cake.

Yahuda What?

Freud Nothing.

Yahuda Freud, you've finally lost your marbles. Sixty years of clinical smut has taken its toll. Cross-dressing, violent tendencies and attempted sodomy . . . I'll keep it quiet of course, but I don't think you'll be publishing much else.

Freud That is slanderous! What proof have you?

Dali Owww.

Yahuda I'll get my bag. When he regains consciousness I shall find out exactly what's been going on here.

Yahuda *exits.*

Freud *close to panic. Knocks on the closet. Lifts* **Dali** *by the ankles. The closet door remains closed.* **Freud** *drops* **Dali** *and knocks again. Lifts* **Dali** *by the ankles. The door remains closed.* **Freud** *goes to the door.*

Freud Open the damn door.

The door opens. He gets **Dali** *by the ankles and slides him towards the closet.*

Freud I gave the signal.

Jessica You hurt my elbow.

Freud Two knocks is the signal.

Jessica That's what you did, and I came out and look at my elbow.

Freud Not one knock, not three knocks; two knocks.

Jessica I'm not having him in here.

Freud He's been rendered harmless. Just a few minutes, please.

Jessica Added to those you already owe me.

Closes door as **Yahuda** *enters.*

Pause.

Yahuda Where is he?

Freud He left.

Yahuda He what?

Freud Through the garden, went over the wall. What a morning. You were right; I should be resting.

Yahuda He was only half-conscious.

Freud Self-induced trance; he uses it to paint.

Yahuda Rubbish.

Freud Exactly. No, you're right. It's rubbish. He was faking. Practical joke. Spanish, of course. Bike all right?

Yahuda What about the underwear?

Freud What?

Yahuda This stuff.

Pulls it from his pocket.

Freud Ah.

Yahuda Well?

Freud What did I say last time?

Yahuda You said it was your daughter's.

Freud Utter nonsense. She's far too . . .

Yahuda I completely concur.

Freud But she's hoping to lose weight. These are a sort of incentive to diet.

Yahuda What sort of a fool do you take me for?

Freud Yahuda. . . . The truth of the matter is. . . . You may laugh, but er . . . you may not even believe it, but er. . . . Well. . . . The Spanish lunatic came early this morning; we had given him permission to paint in the garden. He brought with him a young lady, a professional model . . .

Yahuda It's common knowledge Dali only ever paints his wife.

Freud His wife. She was his wife. The model was. His wife the model. He set up his easel, she unfortunately disrobed. If we had known, it goes without saying . . . They were discovered shortly before you arrived. To save you any embarrassment they were hurried indoors and Dali made a pretence of arriving after you.

Yahuda She's Russian, isn't she?

Freud Wh . . . er?

Yahuda Dali's wife.

Freud She's er . . . is she? Is. Russian, yes.

Yahuda Where is she now?

Freud Oh, she . . . she left. Much earlier.

Yahuda What was she wearing?

Freud Um . . . I give up. What was she wearing?

Yahuda Well not these, for a start.

Freud Well no, but I lent her a jacket and . . . my wellingtons.

Yahuda *eyes the wellington.*

Freud She only took one.

Yahuda I see. And then presumably she hopped half naked all the way down the Finchley Road?

Freud No, she hopped across the lawn to the laburnum bush beneath which she had previously concealed her clothes. Then she left.

Yahuda No one passed me.

Freud Ah, no; they climbed over the wall.

Yahuda What on earth for?

Freud They um, they're in training. They intend to climb a mountain together in the spring. A small Himalayan one. They're very adventurous and very in love.

Yahuda If you say so.

Freud Yes?

Yahuda I'm sure the Himalayas are knee-deep in fornicating Spaniards. Not to mention naked Russians looking for their wellington boots.

Freud Well, apparently so.

Pause.

Yahuda All right, I believe you.

Freud You do?

Yahuda I'd believe anything of the Godless avant-garde.

Freud *collapses with relief.*

Yahuda There's only one more thing you need to explain.

Freud Yes?

Yahuda *wanders to the closet. Raps it once with his knuckles. His hand waves through the air as if to rap again,* **Freud** *stiffens, but the hand becomes an accusing finger.*

Yahuda What's in the closet?

Freud Absolutely nothing.

Yahuda Don't give me that; you've been buzzing around it like a blowfly.

Freud *joins him at the closet.*

Freud Papers, papers, a life's work . . .

Yahuda Open it up.

Freud I've mislaid the key.

Yahuda Open this door.

He raps twice. **Freud** *instantly adds a third rap. Grins inanely.*

Yahuda *frowns, suspicious. Raps twice again.* **Freud** *adds a third rap.*

Yahuda *raps once.* **Freud** *raps twice.*

Yahuda *dummies a rap.* **Freud** *raps twice, then hurriedly adds one.*

Yahuda What in God's name is wrong with you?

Freud *is desperately trying to remember the count.*

Yahuda *raps again, once, and strides away.* **Freud** *in complete confusion adds another one, and also walks away. Then stops dead.*

Freud *Scheisse.*

The closet opens. **Jessica**, *dressed in* **Dali**'s *clothes, walks out. Sees* **Yahuda**'s *back. As she turns, so does he; she attempts to return to the closet.*

Yahuda Ahah! Stop where you are!

She stops.

Yahuda Over the wall is he, Freud?

Yahuda *closes the closet to cut off her escape. She keeps her back to him.*

Yahuda All right, you bohemian buffoon; what have you got to say for yourself?

Jessica *shrugs.*

Yahuda Don't give me any of your continental gestures. Just please inform me what sort of a relationship you have with this man.

Another shrug.

Yahuda Turn around dammit and face me like a man.

Jessica *fiddles with her hair.*

Yahuda I swear he's got shorter.

Jessica *turns round. She's attempted to fashion herself a moustache. A pause.*

Yahuda All right, Freud; over to you. Let's hear it.

Freud Um . . .

Jessica Dr Yahuda, the truth is . . .

Freud You wish to speak to me!

Jessica That's true.

Freud So in order for our conversation to happen, you did not leave with your husband.

Jessica Who?

Freud Dali; your husband. Because you wished to speak to me.

Jessica That's right. I didn't go with my husband Dali, Dali my husband because . . . (*Dreadful Spanish accent.*) . . . I thtayed behind to thpeak to Profethor Freud which ith why I wath thitting in the clothet.

Freud Besides; you'd had a row.

Jessica Ith correct.

Freud And you hit him on the head.

Jessica Thith ith true.

Yahuda With a swan, presumably?

Jessica *Que?*

Yahuda May I ask you a personal question?

Jessica Thertainly.

Yahuda What country do you come from?

Jessica Thpain, of courth.

Freud, *behind* **Yahuda** *now, gestures frantically.*

Jessica Not thpain? No, I hate thpain. Spain. Spain? Plagh!

Yahuda So?

Jessica Sssso . . . I come from . . .

Freud *tries to look like Lenin.*

Jessica A very important city um . . . near Mount Rushmore. No, no. Only joking.

Freud *holds up an umbrella and with his curved arm, tries to make a hammer and sickle.*

Jessica It rains a lot. Where I come from. England, it's . . . no.

He stands in a Russian sort of way.

Jessica The people where I come from are very rugged because it rains so much.

He slow marches.

Jessica In fact many of them are dead.

He tries the same thing again, but more exaggerated.

Jessica Turkey? No. I'm just having you on. If you seriously want to know, um . . .

Freud *stabs at his head with a finger, impersonating Trotsky's death.*

Jessica Where I come from . . . they're all mad. The entire country is completely barmy. France! It's France! I'm French! No, I'm not, what a stupid thing to say.

She's losing her patience with **Freud**, *he's losing his with her. He stands with his finger on his head.*

Jessica Mars. I come from Mars.

Freud *does a Russian dance.*

Jessica Or Russia, I don't give a t . . . Russia! Russia? I come from Russia. That's where I come from. Russia.

Yahuda Really?

Jessica Oh yes. It's very warm for October, isn't it? Precious little snow.

Yahuda You don't sound Russian.

Jessica Oh . . . *Vy mozhete skazat' mnye chuke proiti k zimnemu dvortcu? Dva kilograma svekly i butylku vodki. Da zdravstvuyet velikii Sovetskii Soyuz!* (Can you tell me the way to the Winter Palace? I would like half a pound of beetroot and a bottle of vodka, please. Long live the glorious USSR!)

Freud Oh, bravo.

Yahuda All right, I give up.

Freud That was brilliant.

Yahuda But you came close, Freud, so be warned; I may be willing to suspend my disbelief this far, but not one step further.

Dali *comes out of the closet in his underwear.*

Dali Excuse me please. Dali does not remove his clothings.

Freud I can explain this.

Dali Pretty girls remove their clothings for Dali, not versa vice!

Freud In fact I can, I can explain this.

Yahuda Freud, will you tell me why on earth you are consorting with these lunatics?

Freud Patients, Yahuda.

Yahuda I've been patient long enough!

Freud No, these are my patients.

Yahuda Patients?

Freud My last patients. A couple of mild cases to occupy my mind until . . .

Yahuda I see. Well, you always were one for a challenge, weren't you? Now it all falls into place.

Freud You are a generous and understanding man.

Yahuda Not at all. I'd better leave you to it then. Good afternoon.

Freud Good afternoon.

Yahuda I'll be back of course.

Freud Mmm?

Yahuda You know what for.

Freud *discerns something sinister in these parting words as* **Yahuda** *exits.*

Dali In London the first thing I visit is the famous West End and I see *Look for the Nookie* or somesuch . . .

Freud *Rookery Nook.*

Dali Is so. And I think no; is ridiculous. But in England is like this, and is great fun. So Dali chase you through french windows, round the garden, back through front door, yes?

Jessica No, I don't think so.

Dali You want to kick him again in the reproductives?

Jessica No.

Dali Please.

Jessica I didn't come here for this.

Dali What is this?

Jessica This pathetic farce.

She takes her clothes and goes back into the closet.

Dali Oh. But then you will pose for Dali, yes?

Jessica No.

Dali You think Dali try to seduce you is not true. Dali does not touch. His only passion is to *look.*

Jessica Well, he can look elsewhere.

Dali Your armpit, it is divine. I must make unto it the graven image!

Jessica *emerges, buttoning her dress.*

Dali Where have you hidden it?

Jessica Under my arm. Professor Freud, I wish to continue the analysis.

Freud Whose?

Jessica The one we began.

Freud What is the point? It was concluded years ago.

Jessica Humour me.

Freud The details of the case are fully documented.

Jessica But they're not. Not in your own notes.

She produces a small book.

Jessica This journal belonged to the patient you called Rebecca S. Her real name was Miriam Stein. This is the journal she kept of her work with you.

Freud So?

Jessica I'd like us to read it.

Freud To what end?

Jessica I've simplified what she remembered of the sessions, and selected the most apposite passages. Please; read with me.

Freud I have neither the time nor the inclination.

Dali Please.

Jessica What?

Dali *waves some money at her.*

Dali To consider my request a professional proposition.

Jessica Go to hell.

Dali Is a substantial sum.

Jessica Please.

Freud It's out of the question.

Jessica Why?

Dali Name your price.

Jessica I'm not for sale.

Dali The armpit only. My Venus.

He kisses her hand . . .

Jessica Why not?

Freud It would be a pointless exercise.

. . . and lifts her arm for a peek.

Jessica Get off!

Dali On my knees.

Jessica Pointless?

Dali You see; he begs.

Jessica Are you sure?

Freud I will have nothing to do with it.

Dali Dali will do anything you ask.

Jessica Can you read English?

Dali Dali is perfect English. Not have got you ears?

Jessica Very well. Read the passages underlined.

Dali *Que?*

Freud Look, I really must insist . . .

Dali What for is this?

Jessica We are going to reconstruct one of the Professor's case histories. You sit here. When we are finished you may have fifteen minutes to do what you will with my armpit.

Dali Is a deal. I am to be the fraud of the great Freud, yes?

Dali *sits in the tub seat.*

Freud No. I will not tolerate this.

Dali Ah.

Jessica What anxieties are prompting your objections, Professor? Read the passages marked with an F.

Dali But if the Professor object to this worm presuming to embody him then this Dali cannot possibly . . .

Jessica *puts her hand behind her head.*

Dali . . . refuse you, my darling, and to hell with this man and his beard also.

Freud Very well, if you insist. Get it over with.

Jessica From the top of the page.

Dali So. 'As you speak to me you will notice ideas will occur that you feel are not important, are nonsensical, not necessary to mention. But these disconnected things are the things you *must* mention.' Dali knows this; he has read this from the book. 'You must say whatever goes through your mind. Leave nothing unsaid, especially that which is unpleasant to say.' Maestro.

Jessica Concentrate.

Dali Of course.

Jessica It's a warm day. I had difficulty getting here. The cab driver was reluctant to raise the canopy, and I cannot travel in an open cab.

Dali She knows this; is word-perfect.

Jessica Shut up. Instead of persuading the cabbie, my husband berated me. I had to insist quite firmly, which has made me a little anxious.

She rubs her breast.

Jessica I wish I hadn't come. I don't like leaving the house.

Dali *rubs his nipple exotically.*

Jessica Your line.

Dali *Que?*

Jessica What are you doing?

Dali Is what it says here. I was gently rubbing my breast.

Jessica Not your breast, my breast.

Dali You rub the breast of the patient? Is not in the published works you did this.

He reaches out, she slaps his hand.

Jessica She was rubbing her own breast.

Dali *Que?* Oh, *si*.

Jessica You see?

Dali *Si*.

Jessica 'I' is me.

Dali *Que?*

Jessica 'I' is me.

Dali *Si*. Is obvious, but very bad English.

Freud Listen . . .

Jessica Can we get on!

Dali *Si, si*. So . . .

Jessica I don't like leaving the house. I feel safer inside.

Dali 'I notice you are rubbing your breast.'

Jessica Am I?

Dali 'Yes.'

Jessica I hadn't noticed.

Dali 'Continue.'

Jessica Walking across a field or a town square is a nightmare. I want to stick to the hedge or the edge of the wall, but even then there's this constant possibility. . . . A wicker basket. Just came into my head. Is that the sort of thing?

Dali Is good, no? Apologise. 'Continue.'

Jessica When I was young we had a wicker basket; I used to play ships in it. It was a picnic basket. I don't know why I've thought of this, but . . . my mother reading to us, the story of Chicken Little. A piece of the sky falls on his head. Bits of the sky falling. I hate the sky, the way the clouds scud. Looking through my grandmother's window. There's a birdcage next to me with a canary. It's got some sort of disease; its beak is being eaten away.

Gags.

Jessica Something I've just remembered, God it was horrible, and

I'd forgotten all about it. I'm lying in my grandmother's garden. I'm an adult, I'm nineteen and she's told me to wait for something spectacular. I remember this now. She said if I lay still I'd get a spectacular surprise. And I'm full of anticipation, waiting for her to bring out a cake or something and suddenly . . .

She rubs.

Jessica The air is full of birds. Starlings. Not just a few dozen but thousands. A black cloud of starlings. A tattered sky and those horrible birds just . . .

She gags.

Jessica I run inside. I'm really angry with her. And the starlings roost in trees all round the house and I sit curled up in a cold dark study in a leather chair and listen to the noise and I am terrified. Some of them swoop to the windowsill. My heart races. I'm scared of the starlings. I'm frightened of the birds.

Dali *applauds.*

Jessica Don't do that.

Dali It says this. 'There was applause.'

Jessica *takes the journal.*

Jessica 'There was a pause.'

Dali I see, *si. Si.*

Pause.

Dali In this pause you think maybe I light a cigar?

Jessica No.

Dali No, *si.*

Jessica I don't know why but I'm thinking now of a flame, a small, a candle flame . . . and it's burning *upside down.* I don't understand that. A heavy sky. Leaden. I'm afraid of the sky. No I'm not. It's not the sky, is it? It's that a bird might fly, might pass overhead. Not all those starlings, something far worse; one bird in a blue sky. That's what frightens me. The *possibility* of a bird.

She rubs.

Freud Are you finished?

Jessica No. Later in that same first session, they discuss her eating disorder and she free-associates around food and meals. I haven't learnt this bit. Give it to me.

She reads.

Jessica 'Knife, fork and spoon should be lined up just so. A knife should never be put into the mouth . . . all these rules my father had. Preparing for a picnic . . . the basket! Being allowed to boil the eggs.' And eventually . . . here it is.

Freud Look . . .

Dali Please . . . shhh.

Jessica 'I am about seven years old. I am at the table. My father is giving a dinner party and I have begged to attend. I am on my absolutely best behaviour. The candles are lit and the mahogany shines. I have spooned my soup from the far side of the bowl and I have not spilt a drop. The meat is carved and the vegetables passed. My mother is proud of me. At this point in the analysis I burst into tears and was unable to continue for some time. Dr Freud waited silently. Eventually I was able to recall the rest of the dinner party. I ask my mother to pass the salt. My father disapproves of my using condiments, but I am on my honour to act as an adult. I tip the salt cellar, but nothing comes out. The salt is damp. I shake the salt cellar, only once, and the silver top flies off. Salt pours in a thick quick flow all over my plate, all over my food, and flicks down the table as I try to stop the flow. The guests turn as one to look at me. Some laugh. I feel the most unbearable humiliation. My ears burn. My mother brushes some of the salt into her hand with a napkin, but the food is ruined. So I pick up my knife and fork and I eat it. I pretend it does not taste disgusting. I eat until my mouth is dry, my gums are stinging. Tears of shame and embarrassment spilling and rolling down my cheek. I run upstairs and vomit. Put myself to bed, the bed is cold. I listen miserably to the guests leaving, then my father throws open the door and shouts that I am clumsy, unworthy, a stupid child. I lie in the dark afterwards wondering why he hates me so.' You then announced that the session must come to a close. Then asked, in passing, how often she had intercourse with her husband. She refused to answer. She was pressured to do so.

Freud Where is this leading? What is your point?

Jessica I need to take this step by step. We shall leap to another session; the sixth.

Dali Is great shame. I miss any good bits?

Jessica This is a really good bit.

Freud No. You have told me nothing I do not know.

Dali But is getting to the really good bit.

Freud I refuse to participate any further.

Jessica We're almost there.

Freud Please. Leave.

She opens a desk drawer and pulls out her razor.

Jessica I'm sorry but I have to finish this. Help me finish it.

Dali Please. I say something?

Jessica Yes?

Dali Goodbye.

Jessica Stay where you are.

Dali Just here?

Jessica Just there.

Dali Is good. Is very nice just here. No need to move at all, never.

Freud Put that down.

Jessica Let me do what I have to do and then I swear, I'll disappear.

Freud Very well, but give me the razor.

Jessica No.

Dali Is good to give it to him. Is better to keep it, though. Boy, it's really nice just here, isn't it?

Jessica Sit down. By this time her anorexia has been suspended. She's eating again, quite well. The gagging has greatly reduced; she has successfully related the gagging to the taste of salt, real or imagined, and thus to the trauma of the dinner party. From there.

Dali 'I wish you to concentrate on your fear of birds. What thoughts come to you?'

Jessica The smell of leather. Mahogany. A candle flame. Of course, at the dinner party the candle flames were reflected in the polished wood. They were upside down.

Dali 'What of the birds?'

Jessica Oh, birds, eggs, boiled eggs . . . the picnic basket. I'm sick to death of that picnic bask . . .

Dali 'A pause.'

Jessica I'm eating a boiled egg at a picnic. My whole family is there. My father has refused to undo his collar. It is very hot. He offers me salt in which to dip my egg. I of course decline. I'm in my late teens by now, I think of myself as very demure. I am dressed in white. And there are friends of the family there. This is more than a . . . It was my father's birthday! I feel good towards him. I feel he likes me now. He gives me the odd stiff smile. I wish we were alone; I'm sure we could talk together now. I wish we were alone. A long way off a child is crying. I take a bite of the egg. My father calls my name. Miriam. No! I look up and smile and no!

She cries out in disgust. Rubs violently. Gags.

Dali 'Relax.'

The fit continues.

Dali 'You are here, you are safe. He embraces her.'

The fit continues.

Dali Is your line.

Freud He embraces her!

Dali Oh, *si*. Sorry. Is allowed?

Freud Yes, is allowed.

Dali *embraces her. She passes out, a silent pause, wakes with a scream.*

Jessica No! It's all over me; my dress, my breast.

Dali What is this?

Jessica A bird, a filthy bird. A streak of white, a sudden flash of green, it's warm and wet and it's on my breast. An unspeakable mess; it's bird excrement.

She calms down.

Jessica Without thinking, I wipe at the stuff with my fingers. It makes it worse. It's fluid and pungent, it's everywhere, but especially on my beautiful new . . . breast. And all over my fingers. My father, thankfully, looks away embarrassed. He pretends he saw nothing. I clean up as best I can but my dress is stained and however much I try to clean them, all afternoon my fingers feel . . . sticky. Stuck together. All the way home, I hide my hand. All the way home I can smell it. And my father, all the way home, never once looks at me.

Pause.

Jessica Is that how it was? Her fit?

Dali Was magnificent.

Jessica Is that how it was?

Freud Similar.

Jessica And did you embrace her?

Freud Yes.

Jessica She says . . . (*Reads.*) 'I clung to him to prevent myself falling through the door that had opened up beneath me and through which I had seen that summer's day so clearly. And the door righted itself and I knew it was now my choice to step through and remember whatever I wished. I am so deeply and eternally grateful to this man.'

Freud Transference is common to all successful analyses.

Jessica They all fall in love?

Freud Without exception.

Dali Wow.

Freud And the gift that must be returned is an acceptance of that love, with no love returned, no demands made, no respect diminished.

Jessica You never loved in return?

Freud Of course not.

Jessica She felt euphoric at the revelations tumbling from her past. And the symptoms began to disappear. She recognised the wiping gesture for what it was, and laughed when she caught herself doing it. Life opened up, she said, like a painted fan. What continued to disturb her were your questions about her intimate affairs. She had admitted her distaste for copulation, and acknowledged her husband's frustration. But still every week you pushed, probed and insisted that she spoke of these things.

Freud This is indelicate. I've had enough.

Jessica We've reached the crucial session.

Freud You will leave my house, please.

Jessica What have you to hide?

Freud Don't be impertinent. Whatever confidences you are about to reveal from this poor woman's private reminiscences, and whatever conclusions you may have reached, I can assure you that no impropriety took place between us. And no such impropriety has ever taken place between myself and any patient.

Jessica I'm not accusing you.

Freud But you were about to.

Jessica It's obviously something you feel very defensive about . . .

Freud How dare you!

Jessica But I have no intention of making any such accusations.

Freud Then what is this about?

Jessica One more visit. The seventh. She returns. Things are not good. The gagging has returned and she finds it impossible to keep any food down. Her fingers are useless, and her wiping tic incessant and exaggerated. She's distraught that in spite of all she's learned, she's iller than ever.

Freud When she arrived. Not when she left.

Jessica She was very angry with you, very angry, and you sensed this. Didn't you?

Freud Of course.

Jessica And you encouraged her to express her anger, didn't you?

Freud Of course.

Jessica And did she? Did she? *Did she?*

She hits him.

Dali No.

Freud It's all right. Yes she did.

Jessica I'm almost there. Almost there now.

The hysterical symptoms take hold of her, more exaggerated and more frequent. Other physical tics manifest themselves. She returns to the couch in an increasingly distressed state.

Dali Is what page, which, I don't know.

Jessica *moans loudly, an agonised exhalation that frightens* **Dali**.

Dali Please.

Freud It's all right.

Dali To help me, please.

Freud She's all right. She'll be all right.

He takes the chair.

Freud Rebecca? Rebecca? What is wrong with your hand?

Jessica The excrement.

Freud Your breast?

Jessica And my fingers; covered in shit. I know! I know! But I can't, it's . . . I'm still so angry!

Freud Angry.

Jessica Yes, angry.

Freud At the bird?

She breaks down. Gags.

Freud What is wrong with your mouth?

Jessica The taste.

Freud Describe the taste.

Jessica The taste of salt. It's salt. Everything tastes of salt!! I'm filthy with this shit and all I can taste is salt.

Freud Associate. The taste of salt.

Jessica A candle burns upside down; its reflection in mahogany. The dinner party.

Freud A candle?

Jessica Put it out. No; the . . . cutlery.

Freud Tell me about the candle.

Jessica It's in the middle of the dining table.

Freud No, the other candle.

Jessica What other? There is no other candle. Except the one I was allowed. I hate the dark; my mother allows me a candle. My father thinks it a waste. He will open my door and bark 'put it out'. The door opens . . .

Pause. She's still for a moment.

Jessica Don't put the knife in your mouth. He opens the door. Put out the candle. The taste of salt and my . . . my fingers.

She sobs quietly.

Freud Why are you crying?

Jessica I don't know.

Freud I think you know.

Jessica The candle is burning.

Freud He opens the door.

Sobbing openly, growing in violence..

Jessica He says 'put it out'. Put it . . . ! Put it . . . !

Freud That's enough.

Jessica The candle is not upside down! It's me, I'm upside down! My head is hanging over the side of the bed! Put it . . . !

Freud That's enough now. Rebecca.

Jessica Put it in your mouth!

Incapable of continuing, she stops.

Freud Rebecca. No more now.

Jessica She remembered. She remembered. The mess on her breast and her fingers and the taste of salt.

Dali Don't cry. Please.

Jessica I'm sorry. I'll be all right in a minute.

Dali What was this?

Freud She had remembered being raped. Orally. Before she was five years old.

Jessica The taste of salt was the taste of her father's semen. The filth on her breast that she tried to clean off was his. When she woke in the morning her fingers were stuck together. She had to be carried from your study, and accompanied home. She slept for almost three days.

Freud Over the next few sessions she discarded a great deal of anger and guilt. She regained her appetite and her physical symptoms disappeared.

Jessica She was ecstatic. (*Reads.*) 'For the first time in my adult life I am happy. A simple thing to have been so painfully elusive. I feel there is nothing now in my past that can throw a shadow over my future. This morning I shall prepare . . . a picnic basket.'

Freud However. The events that Rebecca had remembered . . .

Jessica Miriam! Her name was Miriam!

Dali And she and her husband?

Jessica Oh, eventually. Sexual relations were resumed. Which I suppose means *I* also have you to thank, Professor Freud.

Freud What for?

Jessica My life.

Freud She was your mother.

Jessica You cured her.

Freud You have her mouth.

Jessica You released her, enabled her. You were her saviour.

Dali Is good. You come not to criticise, but to pay homage.

Jessica What did you think, Professor?

Freud *lowers his head, thinking.*

Jessica When I found her journal I had to come.

Dali I like this. Your mother is cured and is a happy ending, yes?

Jessica Not really, no.

Dali No?

Jessica Nine years later my mother died in the washroom of an insane asylum near Paris. She took a rubber tube they used for giving enemas and swallowed it; force-fed it to herself. The other end she attached to a faucet, turned the tap and drowned. In case you're still wondering, Professor, that is why I'm here.

Act Two

The same. Twilight.

Dali Is serious now, yes?

Jessica Yes.

Dali I go put my trousers on.

He retires to the closet.

Freud I had no knowledge of your mother's death.

Jessica That's hardly surprising. Rebecca S. has little in common with Miriam Stein. Your patient Rebecca is a successful case history; my mother Miriam a suicidal hysteric.

Freud The last time I saw her was one year after our final session. She returned to inform me of her health and happiness.

Jessica She was pregnant, with me.

Freud She had had, she said, a wonderful year.

Jessica 1897.

Freud What?

Jessica 1897.

An air-raid siren sounds.

Jessica What is that?

Freud A warning, is all.

Frightened, **Jessica** *covers her head with her arms.*

Freud To alert us, not harm us.

Dali *comes out of the closet, crosses and exits out the door.*
Dali Scuse.

Freud *draws the curtains.*
The intercom buzzes.

Freud Yes?

Anna Father? We are going to the shelter.

Freud I'm not. I told you when you built it.

Anna This might not be another drill.

Freud I have been thrown out of my home, shunted over Europe, and shipped across the channel. No further.

Anna It's just down the garden. Fifty yards.

Freud I shall soon be spending a substantial amount of time in a hole in the ground. I don't intend to climb into one while I can still argue the point.

Anna Very well. But keep the curtains closed.

Freud Of course.

Anna And if there are bombs, get under the desk.

Freud Don't be absurd.

He switches it off. **Dali** *enters in a gasmask.*

Dali Scuse.

And goes back into the closet.

Freud If you would prefer to shelter . . .

Jessica No. I prefer to talk.

Freud What were you looking for last night?

Jessica Unpublished notes. Relevant material. I wanted to find out if you knew what you did to her?

Freud I?

Jessica On that final visit.

Freud She was strong, healthy, and functioning well.

Jessica Obviously you *had* managed to turn her into a horse.

Freud Her symptoms had subsided, her neuroses were negligible.

Jessica And my father could penetrate her whenever he so desired. Thank you doctor; my wife is cured.

Freud Not cured no, rendered capable. Remarkably so, considering.

Jessica What?

Freud That her analysis was incomplete.

Jessica Was it? Was it?

Jessica takes a book from the shelf. Opens it at a page she's previously marked.

Jessica The Aetiology of Hysteria. 1896. 'In every case, the cause of hysteria is a passive sexual experience before puberty, ie, a traumatic seduction.' This is what you wrote.

Freud Yes it is.

Jessica No equivocation, no trace of doubt. You wrote to your friend Fliess; 'Have I revealed the great clinical truth to you? Hysteria is the consequence of presexual shock.' That's what you believed.

Freud Yes it is.

Jessica And you published.

Freud Yes I did.

Jessica You were absolutely certain.

Freud Yes I was.

She pulls a crumpled letter from a wellington boot.

Jessica One year later. 'My Dear Fliess. Let me tell you straight away the great secret which has been slowly dawning on me in recent months. I no longer believe in my neurotica.'

Freud What is the point you wish to make?

Jessica Just one year later. And you what, you . . .

Freud A year?

Jessica Change your mind in less than a . . .

Freud The year of my life! 1897 may have been a wonderful year for your mother, but it was torture for me.

Jessica Why?

Freud My clinical cases. I suffered disappointment after disappointment; the analyses refused to come to a satisfactory conclusion; the results were imperfect therapeutically and scientifically. I came to the inevitable conclusion that I was wrong.

Jessica And when my mother returned, smiling, to confide her happiness and my genesis to you . . . you took back your blessing.

Freud At first I believed I had uncovered the inciting trauma. A year later I knew this was not the case.

Jessica You told my mother that her memory of abuse was a fantasy born of desire.

Freud It is more complex than that.

Jessica It's not that complex, Professor. You said her father did not seduce her; that it was she who wished to seduce her father.

Freud That is a gross over-simplification.

Jessica And by the autumn all the childhood seductions unearthed by your patients . . . none of them had ever occurred.

Freud In the unconscious there is no criterion of reality. Truth cannot be distinguished from emotional fiction.

Jessica So you abandoned them.

Freud I abandoned the theory. It was false and erroneous.

Jessica I don't have many vivid memories of my mother. She ate alone; couldn't bear to be seen eating. I never ate a single meal with my mother. I don't remember her treating me badly, but nor do I have the faintest recollection of her loving me. My father had her committed when I was five years old.

The journal.

Freud If we had the time I could help you understand . . .

Jessica There's no need. I understand perfectly. I've spent a long time working to understand this. When you proposed that abuse was the root cause of so much mental illness your movement was at its most vulnerable. You needed the support of the intelligentsia, of institutions, of publishers and instead you were laughed at and reviled. Doors were closed. Anti-Semitic tracts appeared. Everything you'd worked for was threatened.

Freud True.

Jessica Your patients were the daughters and wives of wealthy and privileged men. Whom you began to accuse of molesting their own children. And then suddenly, you decide you were wrong. How convenient.

Freud Convenient? To have shared a Revelation and then discover it was false? All I had to steer myself through that terrible year was my integrity.

Jessica Huh.

Freud I have weathered many storms of protest, but I have never bowed to outrage or to ignorance.

Jessica Had you not changed your mind, the outraged and ignorant would have crucified you!! My own grandfather, who my mother accused, was friend or acquaintance to every publisher in Austria!

Freud You are accusing me of the most heinous opportunism!

Jessica Yes. Yes I am!

Freud Do you realise how many women retrieved 'memories' of abuse while lying there?

Jessica Many.

Freud More than many. You will forgive my astonishment at being asked to believe that sexual perversion was prevalent amidst the genteel classes in epidemic proportions. I was proposing a virtual plague of perversion. Not merely socially unacceptable; fundamentally unthinkable!

Jessica So you thought up something else.

Freud The theory of infantile sexuality . . .

Jessica . . . Is the cornerstone of your entire edifice! Change your mind about that and psychoanalysis would be rubble.

Freud No one has been readier than I to risk our movement in the pursuit of truth.

Jessica My mother . . .

Freud (*harsh*) Your mother was a hysteric! Her memories of seduction were wishful fantasies based on her unconscious desire to possess her father, his penis and his child.

Jessica But my mother . . .

Freud These desires in turn based on her desire to possess her mother, to suckle indefinitely, and to give her a child.

Jessica I've read all this . . .

Freud (*rapid*) A premature rejection of her mother, an unresolved anger at having no penis, a fierce fixation on her father. At the crucial age of seven, if my memory serves me, her mother dies. She believes herself to be guilty of killing her mother to attain her father. Her development is arrested, her guilt repressed along with her desires. Years later she develops the hysterical symptoms and the fantasies begin to emerge alongside the memories.

Jessica But it's all so . . .

Freud Complex.

Jessica All I know is that my mother's father . . .

Freud You know nothing! You are ignorant, presumptuous and obsessed. Your theories are simplistic. Your motives malicious. I have given you quite enough of my time. Thank you.

Jessica Why so angry?

Freud I AM ANGRY WITH NO ONE!

Dali (*off*) Arrgh!

He bursts out of the cupboard, holding his forefinger before him like a beacon. It's bleeding.

Dali Maphu mothur ufgud! Haffmee!

He tears off his gasmask.

Dali Is my blood.

Jessica What have you done?

Dali Please call an ambulance and alert the hospital. Look, is my blood. Is coming out of my finger.

Jessica Calm down, it's not that bad.

Dali Is my blood.

Jessica Have you first aid?

Freud In the drawer. How did you cut yourself?

Dali Is not! I sit in the closet, I notice on the wall the piece of . . . how you say this? Nasal mucus. Fastened to the wall with much exhibitionism. Very old; a previous owner I am sure. Is pearly green with a sharp point that makes a gesture which is a trumpet call for intervention. Is disgusting, so I take my courage, wrap my finger in handkerchief and savagely tear the mucus from the wall! But is hard and steely point like a needle! Look; is here. It penetrate between the nail and the flesh! All the way down.

Jessica All right, calm down.

Dali Is great painful.

Jessica I'm sure it is.

Dali Is to the bone.

Jessica I'll pull it out.

Dali Please. Be carefully.

Jessica *pulls out the mucus. Wraps it in handkerchief.*

Dali Argh!

Jessica Here; disinfect it with this.

Dali Is throbbing.

Jessica Be a brave soldier.

Freud *begins reading his letters to Fliess.*

Dali Is go boom, boom, boom; the music of perfidious infection. Argh!

Jessica What?

Dali Is still there! The pointy part is still deep down. I see it through the nail. Get it out.

Jessica Well, I can't.

Dali Do this!

Jessica It's far too deep.

Dali No! Is, but . . . ! It still throb. Is will be infected. Is death. Death weigh in my hand like ignominious kilo of gesticulating worms.

Jessica It's only a splinter.

Dali Is unknown nasal mucus! This finger is swelled. This hand is begin to rot. Please, get me to a hospital. I have it surgically dismissed at the wrist. Buried. It decompose without me.

Jessica It's not snot anyway.

Dali It's not?

Jessica No, it's not.

Dali *Si si*! It's snot. Is what I said.

Jessica It's a bit of glue.

Dali It's not.

Jessica No. A drop of wood glue.

Dali Oh. *Si*.

Jessica You'll survive.

Dali Is possible. Thank you.

Freud *replacing letters in cabinet.*

Jessica What are you doing?

Freud I'm sorry?

Jessica I haven't read them all yet.

Freud And why should I allow you to examine my personal correspondence?

Jessica Why should you not?

Freud Because it is personal.

Jessica You said things to Fleiss you would never say to others.

Freud Our communications were at times a little unguarded.

Jessica Give them to me.

Freud No.

Jessica Why not?

Freud The discovery of your mother's sad history has been very traumatic for you, but whatever quest you have set yourself is a hopeless one. I have nothing to hide.

Loud knocks from the front door.

Jessica Then let me have the letters.

Freud Indeed, to hide nothing has been my sole quest.

He leaves, taking the letters with him.

Jessica What are you drawing?

Dali Him.

She looks.

Jessica You are a cruel man.

Dali No.

Jessica Then you have cruel eyes.

Yahuda's *voice off, then both enter.*

Yahuda Freud. Apologies for this but I must beg hospitality. Every time I turn on my bicycle lamp I'm yelled at by cockney plebeians in flat caps and armbands. It's pitch black; I can't get home. Ah.

Freud Nor can Mr Dali and his wife.

Dali *looks for his wife.*

Freud Your wife.

Dali Please?

Yahuda We met earlier.

Dali Oh, *si. Si.*

Yahuda How's the training going? Both pretty fit?

Dali Which is this?

Yahuda I got on top of one or two myself when I was younger.

Dali Please?

Yahuda Couldn't keep it up though.

Dali Oh, *si.*

Yahuda The nice thing is, they don't have to be enormous to be satisfying, wouldn't you agree? If you're not used to it, small ones are sufficiently stimulating. How far up her do you hope to get?

Dali This man is a doctor?

Freud I mentioned that you and your wife . . .

Yahuda A word of advice – always use the best quality rope and don't attempt anything vertical the first time.

Dali Please?

Freud That you and your wife much enjoyed mountaineering.

Dali Oh?

Jessica I think it's time Dr Yahuda was told the truth.

Freud No.

Jessica Mr Dali and I are not married.

Freud But share a common-law agreement. It's a changing world, Yahuda.

Jessica We met for the first time earlier this afternoon.

Freud A rapidly changing world.

Yahuda So why were you here in the first place?

Jessica It is true that I am Russian.

Freud Is it? Good.

Jessica And I have been engaged by Professor Doctor Freud to translate some of his letters.

Freud Yes, that's it. Precisely.

Jessica And those are the only ones I haven't done.

Freud Ah.

Jessica May I continue?

Freud No.

Jessica Why not?

Yahuda Why not?

Freud Very well. If you must.

Jessica *takes the letters.* **Freud** *can't let go of them. She pulls, third time lucky.*

Jessica Thank you, Professor.

She retires to read.

Yahuda What's wrong with your hand?

Freud Nothing. Hysterical grip reflex. When I was young I er . . .

Makes a repeated gesture with his wrist. Recognises it as an obscene gesture.

Freud . . . dropped an icecream.

Yahuda *finds the manilla envelope containing the Moses article.*

Yahuda Stamped and addressed, I see. Off to the publishers?

Freud Yes.

Yahuda You realise of course, you have a Moses complex?

Freud I beg your pardon?

Yahuda I read an article. Some woman you once sent barmy. Said you identified with Moses.

Freud Moses is nothing but the flesh of sublimation.

Dali Superb.

He makes a note.

Yahuda It is a bad time to discourage men from putting their faith in God.

Freud On the contrary.

Yahuda Have you read this evening's paper?

Freud No.

Yahuda Then do so.

Slaps it at him.

Yahuda Seven thousand Jewish shops looted. Three hundred synagogues burned to the ground. Babies held up to watch Jews being beaten senseless with lead piping. They are calling it *Kristallnacht*.

Freud *takes the paper.*

Yahuda Apparently Goerring is displeased that so much replacement glass will have to be imported. He said they should have broken less glass and killed more Jews. Have you heard from your sisters?

Freud No.

Jessica Sisters?

Freud Four elderly ladies. We have not been successful in our attempts to bring them out.

Yahuda Don't blame yourself.

Freud It is entirely my fault.

Yahuda No.

Freud If I myself had left sooner, I would have been more able to make suitable arrangements.

Yahuda You've done what you can.

Freud I do not believe I shall see them again.

Yahuda They say it is to be the last war. Do you think so?

Freud My last.

Yahuda *swings the light-pull like a bar skittles game. It knocks over half a dozen figures.*

Yahuda You lead us from the wilderness and then abandon us. If you think you're Moses why for the love of God throw doubt upon him now?

Jessica Why indeed?

Freud Have you finished with those?

Jessica It couldn't mean you with to be doubted, could it?

Freud I wish to be left in peace!

Jessica You doubt nothing?

Freud Nothing!

Yahuda What are you reading?

Freud Nothing.

Jessica You should read them also.

Freud Yahuda. A cigar?

Yahuda You stink of cigars.

Freud No more lectures. I have already smoked myself to death. I now do it purely for pleasure.

Freud *lights a cigar.*

Jessica This one's interesting.

Yahuda Is it?

Freud No, it isn't. Come on, Yahuda. I need some fresh air.

Yahuda What about the Luftwaffe?

Freud You think from two thousand feet, they could spot the butt of an old cigar?

Yahuda With my luck they'll recognise you instantly.

Yahuda *and* **Freud** *exit.*

Jessica It's not a dream then, us being here?

Dali Whose?

Jessica His. If he's not here we can't be a dream.

Dali Strictly speaking is quite possible. All peoples in a dream being representative of the dreamer.

Jessica That's what I told him, that I was a facet. He denied it quite vehemently.

Dali What are you looking for?

Jessica I don't know, but I think he does.

Dali Lift your arm. You owe this.

She does. He draws. She reads.

Dali Later, you and I; we have dinner of seafood. Crush the complacent shell of crab and lobster and eat the flesh while still surprised. Then break into National Gallery and visit the London Exhibition of Degenerate Art courtesy of Adolph Hitler, then tomorrow at dawn, by the light of the sun rising over Primrose Hill I shall render your armpit through my eyes and into history.

Jessica I'm washing my hair.

Dali Heaven, to Dali, is the depilated armpit of a woman.

Jessica Forget it. That's the hair I'm washing. Do you expect to make love to all your models?

Dali Never. Sometimes they make love to one another, but Dali only watches.

Jessica Is that honourable or sad?

Dali Please, do not try to understand Dali. This is only his job, and believe me, is too difficult.

Jessica You don't like being touched do you? I noticed earlier. it makes you anxious. It makes you squirm.

Dali Please.

Jessica Do you make love to your wife?

Dali We did this, but no more.

Jessica Why not?

Dali The last time we made love, Dali, at the climax of his passion, cried out the name of another.

Jessica Your mistress?

Dali No, my own. Gala she say is over, and goes fuck fishermen.

Jessica Does that bother you?

Dali Gala I adore. She is everything. But no, I cannot let her to touch me. Always, I hate to be touched.

Jessica So have I.

Dali Is true?

Jessica Unlike you I find it very painful.

Dali Touching?

Jessica Not touching. I pray I shall not have to live my entire life like this.

He stands, she stiffens, he sits again. She stands and sits beside him. Their hands rise, fall, courting. Finally they hold hands for about four seconds, then let go.

Dali How was it for you?

Jessica Wonderful, thank you.

She moves away, wiping her hand.

Dali You feel the bones too? Is enough sex for Dali. How these ugly millions do this thing to get these gruesome children, all this sucking and prodding and body fluids in and out of one another I will never understand. Inside a beautiful woman is always the putrefying corpse of Dali's passion.

Freud *returns.*

Freud Scrape them off on the rockery! I'll fetch you a shoe brush. Are you finished?

Jessica No. Where's your friend?

Freud He wished to be left alone. He is a good and powerful man. It is hard to see him powerless.

Jessica It is hard to believe in good and powerful men, it is so often a contradiction in terms.

Freud Give me the letters.

Jessica No.

She leaps up and goes into the closet. Pops out again.

Jessica You regret nothing?

Freud Nothing! In my life. Nothing! Except perhaps one inadvisable evening at *Rookery Nook*.

Jessica Don't worry, I shan't be in here forever.

Closes and locks the door behind her.

Freud Then come out for pity's sake! Say what you have to say and leave me alone! Is this me?

Dali No. Is a drawing by Dali.

Freud But is this what I look like?

Dali To Dali, *si*.

Freud I look dead.

Dali Is no offence. Dali sees beneath.

Freud Soon, then.

Dali But before you go. Please. One thing you do for him.

Freud What?

Dali To judge the work of Dali. The world is a whore, there is no one can tell me. Only you.

Freud Your work?

Dali Please. You see, if this is no good in your eyes . . . I have wasted the time of my life. When you look at my paintings, what do you see? Well, you see what I see, obviously, that is the point. But have I caught what we are chasing, you and I? Can you *see* the unconscious?

Freud Oh, Mr Dali. When I look at a classical picture, a landscape, or a simple still life, I see a world of unconscious activity. A fountain of hidden dreams.

Dali *Si?*

Freud But when I look at your work I'm afraid all I see is what is conscious. Your ideas, your conceit, your meticulous technique. The conscious rendition of conscious thoughts.

Dali Then this . . . He . . . I see.

Freud You murder dreams. You understand?

Dali Of course. (*Pause.*)

Freud I hope I've not offended you.

Dali No, no no. Is just the Death of the Surrealist Movement, is all.

Freud Surely not.

Dali Is no matter, but is kaput. You tell me nothing I do not know already. I shall give up the paint.

Freud Oh please, not on account of me.

Dali No, no no . . .

Freud You must continue.

Dali No. No no no. No. All right, I shall continue. You and me, we know is shit, but the world is a whore. She will buy the shit. I shall buy a small island.

Freud Could you spend your life pursuing something you no longer believed in?

Dali Oh yes, no problem.

Jessica *emerges from the closet.*

Freud *is now genuinely frightened of her.*

Jessica I'm ready. I have it now. 1897. Who can tell me what is odd about this sentence? 'Those guilty of these infantile seductions are nursemaids, governesses, and domestic servants. Teachers are also involved, as are siblings.' Well?

Dali Give us a clue.

Jessica If you like.

She finds another letter.

Jessica 'The old man died on the night of October 23rd, and we buried him yesterday.' This was your father. 'He bore himself bravely, like the remarkable man that he was. By one of the obscure routes behind my consciousness his death has affected me deeply. By the time he died his life had been long over, but at death the whole past stirs within one.'

Freud Give them to me.

Jessica No. Nursemaids, governesses, servants, siblings . . . no mention of fathers, Professor?

Freud I've had enough of your inquisitory meanderings.

Jessica I need look no further! I know why you changed your mind. Another letter to Fliess, justifying your decision. Pleading your seduction theory could not stand up because 'In every case of hysteria the father, *not even excluding my own*, had to be blamed as a pervert'. Not even excluding my own!

Freud My father was a warm-hearted man possessed of deep wisdom.

Jessica And?

Freud I loved and respected him.

Jessica And.

Freud This is preposterous.

Jessica An earlier letter. 'I have now to admit that I have identified signs of psychoneuroses in Marie.' Who was Marie? Marie was your sister.

Freud The error into which I fell was a bottomless pit which could have swallowed us all.

Jessica Perhaps it should have done. You suspected your father.

Freud That is quite enough.

Jessica Your family leave for the summer, you stay alone. You embark on your own self-analysis.

She flicks pages.

Freud Those letters are private.

Jessica Analyse this sentence, Professor Freud. 'Not long ago I dreamt that I was feeling over-affectionate towards Matilde (my eldest daughter, aged nine) but her name was Hella and I saw the word Hella in heavy type before me.' I looked up the name. Hella means Holy. You desired that which was holy to you.

Dali No. No more. This is a great man. It takes one to know one, which is proof.

Jessica Your mind was in turmoil! The year your father died you found him condemned out of your own mouth. And then you realised your own potential for complicity in such things. Your own daughter.

Freud There was no desire. The dream fulfilled my wish to pin down a father as the originator of neurosis.

Jessica Then you admit you suspected . . .

Freud My *wish* to do so!

Jessica And yet the year of his death . . .

Freud I suspected nothing.

Jessica The year of your own analysis . . .

Freud Do not presume . . .

Jessica You choose to denounce your own theories!

Freud I had no choice!

Jessica Other than denounce your own father! Other than denounce yourself!

Dali No! You, miss-prissy-kiss-my-armpit-tight-arsed-girlie say this slanderous things no more!

Jessica It only remains for me to make my findings known.

Freud To whom?

Jessica I believe Dr Yahuda may lend a sympathetic ear.

She exits into the garden.

Freud Come back here!

Jessica Dr Yahuda!

Dali She is cast aspersions on integrity of all great men!

Freud Stop her.

Dali She is need have her head examined!

Freud Bring me those letters.

Dali Is a pleasure! Dali, he Look for the Nookie!

Dali *pursues.* **Yahuda** *enters through the DS door.*

Yahuda I've mislaid my gasmask. Did I leave it in here?

Freud I've not seen it.

Yahuda Maybe on the porch.

Freud No. I think I saw it in the hall.

Yahuda I've looked in the hall.

Freud I'll look with you.

The sound of breaking glass.

Yahuda What's that?

Freud Nothing. I'm not sure. Probably just a . . . bomb.

Yahuda A bomb!?

Freud Very likely.

Yahuda Highly unlikely.

Freud Unexploded. So far. I suggest we take immediate refuge.

Yahuda In the shelter?

Freud No! Under the stairs.

Yahuda Under the what?

Freud *hustles* **Yahuda** *out of the door.* **Jessica** *enters through the window. Scrunching through broken glass off.*

Dali (*off*) You think it discourage Dali you wield at him the greenhouse? No! Scabrous little non-fornicating fantasists like you Dali will squeeze between his fingernails!

Jessica *notices the buff envelope on the desk. An idea comes to her. She removes the* Moses and Monotheism *text from the envelope and puts the* Fliess *letters in its place, resealing the envelope. The other text she puts in the maroon file.*

Dali (*off*) You must learn to respect for betters and olders and men who struggle in the mind like a silly girl could not begin to do!

As **Jessica** *finishes,* **Dali** *bursts in holding a length of hemp rope.*

Dali Is swing, from tree. You want to give me papers and shut up and be good girl, or I do this worst thing to you.

Jessica *picks up a phallic stone figure.*

Jessica Try it.

Dali What a woman. Is heavy, no?

Jessica Yes.

Dali So. I am fearless, *si?*

Dali *takes a step forward,* **Jessica** *swings the figure, he cowers.*

Dali Donta hita the head! Is full of precious stuff!

Enter **Freud**.

Freud Move the Ewbank and tuck yourself well in.

Yahuda (*off*) This is absurd.

Freud I'll find your mask.

Closes the door behind him.

Dali Dali is got her but she grow violent, so best cure her quickly, *si?*

Jessica There's nothing wrong with me.

Dali Put this down or be warned.

Jessica Go to hell.

Dali OK. OK. You push Dali to employ his superior intellect!

He picks up a similar but much larger figure.

Freud That is four thousand years old!

Jessica What about this one?

She throws hers at **Dali**

Freud Catch that!

Dali *catches it but drops his own on his foot.*

Dali Argh!

Jessica *runs out of the french windows.*

Jessica Dr Yahuda!

Dali All right, now is personal.

Dali *pursues* **Jessica**, *taking a really big figure.* **Freud** *picks up the maroon file and goes to the filing cabinet.*

Freud *changes his mind, crosses to the stove, opens the lid, and drops the file in the fire. The fire roars.*

Yahuda *enters.*

Yahuda What do you want?

Freud Nothing.

Yahuda Not you; her.

Freud Who?

Yahuda I heard shouts.

Freud For the warden. There is a large unexploded bomb in the greenhouse.

Jessica (*off*) I need your help, Yah . . . (*Hand clamped over her mouth.*) . . . huda!

Yahuda There, you see?

Freud No, no. Our local warden is Mr Yahoohaa.

Jessica (*off*) Yahuda!

Yahuda I distinctly heard my name.

Freud Nonsense. It's all in my head. Your head.

Yahuda Was that a Freudian slip?

Freud Certainly not.

He trips over the rug.

Freud Excuse me. I must . . . the bomb.

He picks up a soda syphon and exits into the garden. **Yahuda** *spots the buff envelope and picks it up. Unable to restrain himself, he takes it to the stove and hesitates.*

Jessica (*off*) Dr Yahuda!

This spurs **Yahuda** *to action. He lifts the lid.*

Jessica *enters, her head bleeding, and tied round the waist by a rope. On the end of the rope, attempting to restrain her,* **Freud** *and* **Dali**.

Jessica Oh, thank Go . . . no! Don't do that!

Yahuda I was er . . . warming my hands!

Jessica What's that envelope doing in them?

Yahuda Good grief; thank God you spotted that.

Freud How dare you!

He takes the envelope from **Yahuda**.

Freud Have you no regard for a man's life work?

Yahuda Life's work? Senile piffle.

Jessica There's something you must know. The story of infantile sexuality is based upon . . . (a false premise!)

Freud *puts a gasmask on her.*

Freud This woman has turned violently psychotic.

Jessica *yells her findings unintelligibly.*

Freud In extreme cases I'm afraid only extreme methods will suffice.

Jessica *tries her best.*

Freud You see; senseless ramblings.

Dali Please to calm down like the good little girl should be seen and not heard.

Jessica *gives up.*

Freud But you, Yahuda; you should be ashamed of yourself. A man's words are his legacy. They should not be censored or selectively distorted. They should stand in their entirety as a monument to his human fallibility and to his . . .

Checks the contents.

Freud . . . Aahg! No, you're right, let's burn the damn stuff.

Jessica No!

Yahuda Bravo!

She grabs it. **Dali** *tries to get it off her.*

Dali Leave this things alone now; is none of little girl's business.

Freud Give it to me!

Jessica Yahuda . . . read this.

She gives the envelope to **Yahuda**.

Yahuda What?

Jessica Read it. Read it!

Yahuda I've already read it.

Freud *takes the envelope.*

Freud It has been a very stimulating afternoon, but I must ask you all to leave now.

Freud *goes for the door. He pulls the handle, but the door has become rubber-like. It bends without opening.*

Freud Good God.

Dali How you do this?

Freud What's going on?

Dali Do it again.

Jessica Don't let him destroy the letters.

Yahuda What?

Jessica The envelope; don't let him burn it.

Freud *uses the intercom.*

Freud Anna!

Dali *tries the door.*

Dali Is fantastic.

Freud Anna!

From the intercom a **Child**'s *scream.*

Child No, Papa! No!

And a **Father**'s *solemn reprimand.*

Father Sigmund.

Freud No.

Turns off the intercom and retreats in fright.

Yahuda What was that?

Freud Nothing. You heard it?

Jessica I will not be silenced.

Freud You will leave this house.

Jessica I shall go to the papers.

Freud I shall call the police.

Jessica I shall publish the letters.

Freud *picks up the phone. It turns into a lobster.*

Freud Hello? Would you please connect me with . . . aaaargh!

Yahuda What the hell is going on here?

Dali Don't look at me.

Freud, *frightened now, goes for the door, thinks better of it, heads for the french windows.*

Freud Everything's fine. But reluctantly I must bring the evening to a close.

He opens the curtains. A train is hurtling across the garden towards him. Steam, bright lights glaring straight ahead, and a piercing whistle.

Freud Arrgh!

Yahuda What the devil?

Freud *closes the curtains.*

Yahuda What was that?

The clock strikes. **Freud**, *terrified, compares his watch. The clock melts.*

Yahuda What's happening?

Dali Is the camembert of time and space, no?

A deep, dangerous, thunderous music begins, low at first, building. The edges of the room begin to soften.

Jessica Dr Yahuda, you have to hear me, before it's too late.

Freud No!

Yahuda Are you all right?

Freud Please, Yahuda . . .

Yahuda You look unwell.

Freud Go home.

Yahuda I'm your physician, Freud, not another figment of your addled imagination.

Freud But if you were it would please me most to imagine you sitting by the fire with a good book . . . *at home.*

Yahuda *disappears through a trap door, or in a puff of pantomime smoke.*
Jessica *gets a hand free and tears off the mask.*

Jessica Dr Yahuda!

Freud Gone! Ha, ha!

Jessica Then I shall go too. And find someone willing to listen.

Freud No. No. I'm getting the hang of this now. You are nothing more than a neurotic manifestation . . .

Jessica Of what?

Freud Of a buried subconscious . . . of a . . .

Jessica What?

Freud You don't exist. I can't hear you.

Jessica Of a what?

Freud The vaguest sense . . .

Jessica Of what?

Freud Of g . . . Get out of my head! House! Head!

The room continues to melt.

Dali Back in the closet and there to stay.

Jessica Let me go!

She kicks **Dali** *in the crotch and dashes out of the DS door. He dives for and catches the rope.*

Dali Is no panic. He is got her!

Jessica's *momentum pulls him out of the room.*

Freud And stay out.

But **Dali** *reappears almost instantly, pulling the rope.*

Dali Is OK. She not got anywhere.

Freud Let her go.

Dali I bring her back.

Freud No!

Dali Is no problem.

Freud Just . . . let the rope go.

Dali You and me we sort this woman out once and for all, *si*?

Freud No, please . . .

Dali Come back here, you hysterical bitch!

Freud Please, don't . . .

Dali *gives an almighty tug.* **Jessica** *is no longer tied to the rope. Into the room spills a nude* **Woman**. *Glittering music.*

Freud No.

Dali Who is this?

Freud No, please . . .

The woman moves towards **Freud**; *he is both attracted and repelled.*

Dali Is fantastic! But is who?

Freud Matilde?

Woman Papa.

Freud No. Matilde?

The **Woman**, *embraces* **Freud**.

Woman Papa.

Freud Oh, my Matilde.

The embrace turns sexual.

Freud No.

Dali Is the most desirable, no?

Freud No! Don't touch me!

He disengages.

Freud I never . . . ! I never even imagined . . . !

Woman Papa!

Freud Leave me alone!

He runs to the window. She pursues him. Train whistles, and curtains billow. **Freud** *tries to hide in the closet. Opens the door and through it topples a cadaverous, festering, half-man, half* **Corpse**. *Screeching music.*

Freud Ahhh!

Dali Aaaargh!

Corpse Sigmund!

Freud God help me.

The **Corpse** *pursues* **Freud**. **Dali**, *in terror, climbs onto the filing cabinet.*

Woman Papa!

Sounds of shunting trains compete with music; a drowning cacophony. Grotesque **Images** *appear, reminiscent of* **Dali**'s *work, but relevant to* **Freud**'s *doubts, fears and guilts. More* **Bodies** *appear on the rope, the* **Bodies** *reminiscent of concentration camp victims, as are the antique figures being scattered by the* **Woman** *and the* **Corpse**. *Distant chants from the Third Reich. Four* **Old Ladies** *make their way to a gas chamber.*

Ladies Sigmund. Siggy. Sigmund.

Heads hung, they undress . . .

Freud *is horrified as the contents of his unconscious are spilled across the stage.*

Dali *is hit by a swan. Suddenly there appears a huge, crippled, faceless* **Patriarch**. *He enters and towers over* **Freud**. *Music descends to a rumble.*

Jessica *enters, searching blindly*

Freud Papa?

Jessica Mama?

Woman Papa?

Jessica Mama?

Corpse Sigmund!

The **Patriarch** *lifts his crutch and swings it, striking the cowering* **Freud** *a massive blow on the jaw.* **Freud** *screams in agony and collapses.*

Jessica Mama? Mama? Mama?

Jessica *is grasped and awkwardly embraced by the figure. Her eyes are screwed shut so as not to see his face.*

Patriarch Open your eyes.

Jessica *shakes her head.*

Patriarch Open your eyes. Then I shall open them for you.

The razor appears in his hand and he cuts open one of her eyes.

Music crashes. Lights crash to a tight downlight on **Freud**. *Stillness. Silence.*

Freud Deeper than cancer. The past. And of all the years, the year I looked into myself, is the year that has been killing me. In the months of May and April, one by one, I hunted down my fears, and snared them. Throughout the summer, mounted, pinned and labelled each of them. In October, my anger, for the most part, I embalmed. And in December I dissected love. Love has ever since been grey and lifeless flesh to me. But there has been little pain. The past, for the most part, has passed. I chose to think, not feel.

Dali *leans into his light, smiles.*

Dali Better now?

Freud Am I dying?

Dali *Si.*

Freud And all this?

Dali Don't blame me for this; is nothing to do with. I tell you already; surrealism is dead. Besides; is impossible to understand.

Dali *gestures. The* **Patriarch**, *the* **Woman**, *the* **Corpse** *and the* **Old Ladies** *all disappear. The set begins to return to normal.*

Freud What about you?

Dali Dali? Is true. He visit you. This was two months ago. And he look at the death in your face of Freud and he understand how many things were at last to end in Europe with the end of your life. But apart from this he visit and . . . nothing happens much.

Freud Yahuda?

Dali Many Jews.

Freud Her?

Dali She is nothing. Please. (*He sits* **Freud** *in his chair.*) So . . . Dali visits. Freud remembers . . . sleeps. Goodnight.

Exit **Dali**.

The air-raid all-clear siren sounds. The set completes its return to normal, as do the lights. **Jessica** *stands looking at the sleeping* **Freud**.

Jessica Professor?

His eyes open.

Jessica Were you sleeping?

Freud I don't believe so.

Jessica I'm sorry I got angry.

Freud To get angry is most necessary.

Jessica Better out than in?

Freud Certainly.

Jessica But what about those that get hurt?

Freud If the anger is appropriately expressed . . .

Jessica What about the children?

Freud No-one gets hurt.

Jessica Ha!

Freud It is painful to understand one's complicity in these things.

Jessica Do you still insist my mother was never molested by my grandfather?

Freud No, she was not.

Jessica Well, that's a remarkable thing.

Freud Why?

Jessica Because I was. And please don't suggest that I imagined this. He was no beloved, half-desired father to me. He was a wiry old man who smelt of beer and cheese and would limp to my bed and masturbate on me. Only once was it an unexpected thing. And once, he whispered that if I told my father, he would do worse to me with this.

She shows the razor.

Jessica My mother knew what he would do, if she were not there to listen for the door, the creaking stair. That's why she protested at being sent away. And so fierce and vehement her protest, sent away she surely was.

Freud *bows his head.*

Jessica What was it you remembered in your self-analysis, Professor? About your father?

Freud What is more relevant is what I could not remember.

Jessica Have you no feelings?

Freud I chose to think. And if now I am not so much a man as a museum, and my compassion just another dulled exhibit, so be it. All I have done, what I've become . . . was necessary. To set the people free.

Jessica Dead already.

Freud Oh, a few bats hang like heartbeats in the tower. Fear. The odd rat still scampers through the basement. Guilt. Other than that the building is silent.

Jessica Liar.

Freud I hear nothing.

Jessica You heard me.

Freud Nothing.

Jessica Listen harder.

Freud *breaks down. Weeps.*

Jessica What? What is it?

Freud The exhibits are screaming.

She comforts him briefly.

Jessica Goodbye.

Freud I don't know your name.

Jessica Jessica.

Freud God is looking.

Jessica Goodbye.

Freud Jessica. The young may speak what the old cannot bear to utter.

Jessica Because I can articulate these things does not mean I am able to bear them.

She leaves. **Yahuda** *enters and examines the chessboard.* **Freud** *speaks with difficulty.*

Freud Yahuda?

Yahuda Freud?

Freud You will remember you promised to help me when the time came. Well, it's torture now.

Yahuda *nods.*

Yahuda Have you spoken to Anna?

Freud She will understand.

Yahuda *nods. From his bag he takes a hypodermic, prepares it, and injects* **Freud** *with two centigrammes of morphine.*

Freud Thank you, my friend. On the desk. There are some carbons . . .

Yahuda Which, these?

Freud To Fliess.

Yahuda I have them.

Freud The one on the top.

Yahuda Yes?

Freud Take a pen. A pen; use ink. Find 'The fathers'.

Yahuda Yes?

Freud Delete for me the five words that follow. 'Not even excluding my own.'

Yahuda Done.

Freud Illegible?

Yahuda Gone.

Freud Thank you.

He closes his eyes. Grimaces.

Yahuda I shall repeat the dose in twelve hours' time. Two centigrammes, a little more, whatever's called for. You may hallucinate. Don't be afraid.

The grimace tightens, then the drug takes hold.

Freud Oh . . . heaven.

*And **Freud**'s face relaxes as he falls into a sleep which will become his last.*

Yahuda *dismisses a tear, takes a last move at the chessboard and leaves quietly.*

The sound of rain beyond the window, and a subtle change of light.

Freud *wakes. Looks at his watch.*

Freud If you arc waiting for me to break the silence you will be deeply disappointed. The silence is yours alone, and is far more eloquent than you might imagine.

He turns in his chair and looks towards the couch. Frowns when he sees there is no one on it.

Jessica *appears through the rain and stops outside the french windows. Her hair hangs dripping to her shoulders.*

She taps on the glass. **Freud** *looks at her. Closes his eyes, too tired to go through all this again, but knowing he may have to.*

Jessica *continues to tap as the lights fade.*